A SEED OF LOVE

CHERYL LEE HARNISH

First Edition

Copyright © 2011 Cheryl Lee Harnish

To contact the author please visit her website: www.FractalArt.ca

Editor: Arlene Prunkl
Associate Editor: David Emery
Cover Artwork: "Seeds of Love" © Cheryl Lee Harnish
Headshot Photography: © Mark Brennan

Library and Archives Canada Cataloguing in Publication

Harnish, Cheryl Lee, 1970-
A seed of love / Cheryl Lee Harnish.

Includes index.
ISBN 978-0-9783047-1-3

1. Mental healing. 2. Spiritual healing. 3. Guides (Spiritualism).
4. Depression, Mental. I. Title.

RZ401.H37 2011   615.8'52   C2011-901120-4

MIX
Paper from
responsible sources
FSC
www.fsc.org   FSC® C004071

Printed and bound in Canada

DEDICATION

This book is lovingly dedicated to my father,
Donald Michael Harnish

SPECIAL THANKS

Brent, Brandon, Jaden, and Mom
your love is the reason I am who I am today.
Peter Stathis and Tracey Smith
for your friendship and support over the years...
I treasure you both.

"The Real You — the very core of You — is untouchable, unstoppable, and unlimited. And if you gave yourself permission to allow even the smallest ray of your Inner Light to glisten unimpeded, you would illuminate this world far greater than any sunrise ever could."

~ Cheryl Lee Harnish
(from The Greatest Mystery video)

CONTENTS

ᴖᴖᴖ Introduction ᴖᴖᴖ

Finding our true path and right place in life isn't always easy. There are times when we need support, encouragement, and guidance in our lives. This is my story of how I discovered my path, my gifts, and my place in this world, and the help I received along the way—both human and divine. To the best of my ability, I have shared my experiences as accurately as I could recall.

The names and identities of certain individuals have been changed for their privacy. In a few places throughout the story, certain details may seem vague—again, this was only to ensure privacy where required.

During the editing and review process of this book, I was questioned as to why I didn't mention my children more or share what was happening for them during my experiences. My reasons are simple. This is the story of my spiritual journey—of finding my path and true place in life.

I love and cherish my children very much, and as a family, we chose to keep this part of our lives private. My children deserve their privacy and their personal experiences are not directly relevant. So in the best interest of my two beautiful boys, this part of our lives will not be shared. I had to follow my heart on this.

As you will soon discover, I share many situations throughout my adventures when I am called to follow my heart—regardless of what anyone else thinks. I strongly believe that our hearts are the most important tool we have been given. They guide us on our way. Even though it wasn't planned, it is very suiting that the book begins here with the same theme found throughout the rest of the story—follow your heart.

1

Into the Light

I recognized this buzz of fidgety energy as it moved throughout my body—without question, it was resistance to the process. For some reason, I had a really hard time being hypnotized. This was my fourth hypnotherapy session, and I still had to fight myself to let go. It was all I could do to simply lie there, stretched out on a sofa in the living room of my therapist's home. I was about to allow someone into my most private world—my mind.

With my eyes closed, I had nothing else to focus on except her voice and the feelings in my body. The couch was pretty comfortable, I had to admit. Her voice was also pleasant to listen to. That wasn't the problem here. The problem was that I didn't trust anybody. I wanted to trust her, to let go and get into the process. I wanted the healing I knew I could have, if I could just let go. Years of hard knocks, however, had taught me to never trust anyone—ever. This whole process was going against my self-defined rules of survival.

Oh Cheryl, what is your problem? You are paying this woman good money to get into your head, so let her in your damned head already! You do want this, you do. I tried to talk myself through it. This was always the hardest part for me, getting my body to relax. On a deep, cellular level, I knew my body and mind were tied together. If I could just allow all the tension and stress in my body to fade away, as the hypnotherapist instructed, then I'd have to allow my protective wall of control to fade away as well. But if I wasn't in control, then who would be? Could I really trust this woman? Should I trust her? I didn't even know her. Was she going to have my best interests at stake as she rummaged around in my subconscious?

For crying out loud, Cheryl, just shut up and breathe. There is no other way. You've tried everything else. You don't want to live with it anymore, right? And nothing else has worked, right? Okay, so shut the hell up and do what she says. I turned my attention back to the lulling voice guiding me through the process of relaxation.

As I followed the voice and the soothing instructions, I was gradually able to let go into a physically relaxed state. One by one, each muscle released its hold. Rhythmically and soothingly, the voice drew me in more deeply. As my state of awareness began to change, I became acutely aware of my body. I noticed how comfortably it sunk into the well-used sofa, as if it was made perfectly for my form alone. Every muscle was loose and limp. My chest unexpectedly released a large sighing breath, sinking my awareness even deeper down into that comfortable place between consciousness and dreaming. My arms felt heavy too, much too heavy to lift and much too comfortable to care.

This inner realm was a very pleasant place to be. I'd always loved meditating and this was very similar. The only difference was that I was in much deeper than I could ever go with meditation alone. My body enjoyed the well-deserved reprieve from the continual tensing and contracting that my endless onslaught of thoughts created.

I knew this inner place well. Even as a child I had come here a lot. Although most of my childhood memories had hidden themselves away from any hope of conscious recollection, this I remembered clearly. I would barricade myself away in the bathroom, the only place where I could lock a door and create a safe barrier between me and the utter chaos that was my family.

Happy to have a quiet retreat, I would perch myself up on the toilet and close my eyes. I always used the same set of thoughts to create the escape. *What would there be if there was no me?* Once my mind settled into the absence of self, the next question would follow. *What if there was no world?* After a short time, for some reason I couldn't fathom, I usually ended up in outer space. Then the final question would come. *What if there were no stars and universe?*

It worked every time, and I would be taken to a place of complete and utter nothingness. No me, no thoughts, and no existence. It was a place of peace. No God to be angry at. No siblings to fear. No fighting parents. No painful world to deal with. There was absolutely nothing there except an awareness of the nothing—and peace.

I often used this same technique at night to lull myself into sleep. At night, however, I'd usually have a strange perception of size. I'd feel huge and expanded, as though my tiny seven-year-old body was filling the entire space of the room. My arms and legs felt thick and wide, yet very light at the same time. Every tiny cell of my body would become enormous and I would feel as though I were floating. Some nights it seemed possible that I might actually crush my little sister with my hugeness, as she lay asleep beside me.

As I lay on the sofa in the hypnotherapist's office, I embraced the idea of going to my inner place of escape. It was a place only I could go and I did truly love it there. The therapist's presence didn't matter; she wasn't actually in my mind with me, and that was what mattered. I still had complete ownership of my inner world. It was all I needed to finally relinquish control. I allowed my conscious mind to drift away.

I was surprised at how deeply I had gone into hypnosis this time—probably the deepest yet. Interestingly, it wasn't like sleep at all. It wasn't like I didn't know what was happening around me—

quite the opposite, actually. I became acutely aware of everything, especially sound. Even the lightest noise, like the movement of a pen on paper, was clearly audible. I turned my attention over to the voice that was asking me now to go back, far back to the time before I was born, when I was in my mother's womb.

"I'm not that deep. I can't go there," I replied with my usual stubbornness. I *was* actually in deep enough, but I always became just a bit more defiant when I was under hypnosis. I figured it was similar to drinking, where the alcohol clouds your ability to be sensible. For me, hypnosis was something like that.

"Yes, you can," she assured me with confidence. "I'm going to count backwards from three to one. When I reach one I'm going to snap my fingers, and when I do you are going to find yourself back in time, all the way back to the time just before your birth. You are going to find yourself inside your mother's womb. Three—two—one. And be there now."

Snap! The sound of her middle finger sliding off her thumb in a sideways motion created a sharp crack. Within moments, I found myself drifting in darkness. As feelings started to bubble up within me, a large wave of resistance washed through me. These were feelings I did not want to feel.

I really didn't want to be in this place, in my mother's womb. I wanted to argue with the therapist that we shouldn't be doing this, it was useless. But I knew better—anything I resisted this much held something very powerful in my healing process. I knew exactly what all this was pointing to. It was directly linked to my depression.

I had struggled with depression for as long as I could remember being alive. When I was a child, it manifested differently from the adult form. I was no more than five when I first started my conversations with God. My family was not religious; my father dabbled in esoteric studies like ESP, séances, and extraterrestrials, but there was never a mention of God in my home. I'm not sure why I was so obsessed with talking to this Almighty Presence all the time. Maybe I figured if I could just convince God that I was very, very sorry for whatever it was I had done, He would stop punishing me. I felt sure that God would only give someone who was very bad a life like mine.

"Please, please take me back to Heaven," I'd beg of Him. "I don't want to be here. I'm all alone and I don't like it here, pleeeease...I promise I'll be good. Please don't make me stay here anymore. I'll be good the whole rest of the day, you'll see. And when I show you I am good, you can take me back, okay?"

But my begging and pleading never worked. God wasn't going to take me back. I was stuck in this hell-forsaken place and I was on my own. My feelings of disappointment with this Mighty Creator who had all but left me here to rot only grew deeper as I got older.

The first time I attempted suicide I was twelve years old. Looking back, it was a desperate cry for help. It was a good thing I didn't have any solid knowledge of anatomy at the time or I would have succeeded in severing my vein. The last attempt I made at removing myself from the planet was at the age of twenty-four. That one earned me a lovely two-week holiday on the psychiatric ward at the local hospital. As though an entire lifetime of counselors, psychologists, and mental health workers wasn't enough, I now had to face a daily parade of know-it-all, drug-pushing psychiatrists and medical students in training.

In the end, I received a diagnosis of obsessive–compulsive disorder, accompanied by a mild form of the bipolar disorder, manic depression. I wasn't too pleased with that. I thought it was ridiculous and almost humorous. I didn't exhibit any of the signs you normally think of when you hear about OCD. I didn't wash my hands twenty times a day, and I didn't run to check the stove throughout the night. I didn't do any of that. What I did do, though, which earned me a certificate in crazy, was follow the compulsion to do something when I felt strongly enough about it. The things I did often didn't make sense to the people around me, but they made sense to me and that's all I cared about.

To the white coats, that made no sense. Their opinion was that following inner knowings over logic definitely required medical intervention and a diagnosis. I also didn't agree with the manic part of the depression diagnosis either. I thought "chronic" or "severe" was a better description; "manic" seemed a little over the top to me. But who's going to let a patient in the psych ward make their own diagnosis?

I tried to explain that much of it stemmed from my childhood, and the trauma from those days still lingered in me. I tried to explain that my father had committed suicide when I was thirteen. He felt it was the only way to finally conquer the demon the alcohol had become. I rationalized that it had been imprinted on my brain and had become a learned response to failure. But they weren't buying it.

I was condemned to a lifetime of Lithium and anti-depressants. But they didn't work for me at all; being on Lithium was one of the single most horrific experiences I have ever had to endure. It numbs the mind, emotions, and spirit. When that drug was in my system I was a drone, not a human.

A friend of mine who had also taken Lithium came up with an analogy that described it well. You're at the breakfast table with your family and your toast has just popped. You reach out, place the toast on your plate, and pick up your butter knife. At that moment, a nuclear bomb drops to the ground just outside of town. Your entire house shakes violently and the windows blow out all around you. You look around at the others blankly, then say, "Pass the butter, please." Taking Lithium, you become completely numb to everything. However, if I wanted to keep custody of my six-year-old son, I needed to remain on medication during the follow-ups from child services. So only while I had to, I took the damned Lithium.

I was here today on this couch as a last resort. Although it had been over ten years since I'd tried to take my life and I was now living medicine free, I still felt disconnected. Thoughts of ending my life plagued me—I just didn't act on them now. I tried to be happy. I had an incredible husband and a second son now, and we lived on a horse farm just outside of town. I should be happy, but I wasn't. I just couldn't shake the constant feeling of having no purpose. I had no reason to be here. I truly felt I didn't serve any use and it wouldn't make one shred of a difference if I were gone.

Yet somewhere deep inside me, I knew how I felt was wrong, and I didn't want to live like that anymore. I'd had enough. I knew my resistance to going back to my mother's womb was telling me there was something important here to my healing. I had done more than enough personal growth work over the years to know that resistance was simply my ego holding me back.

The ego is the small mind, and it wants us to remain small too. It needs to rule and does its best to keep the Higher Self out of the picture using whatever means possible. Resistance is a common technique of the ego to keep us from connecting to that which can ultimately empower us. I knew this was one of those ego moments.

I breathed deeply. It was during moments like this that my tenacious nature served me in a positive way. I did what was asked of me and I returned to my mother's womb. Although it was emotionally wrenching, I was gaining tremendous insights. I began to feel more at peace now with what had once plagued me. I could actually feel a lightness in my chest.

A few minutes passed, and my experience of being in the womb began to change. I found myself in a different place now, and it wasn't here on Earth. There was something heavy resting on me, on my left-hand side, that I couldn't remove. What was happening? I began to explain out loud what I was seeing and feeling. I almost couldn't believe what I was experiencing.

I noticed a slight tension in the room. Then ever so quietly, Lorraine Bennington, my therapist, lifted herself out of her chair. I heard the distinct flick of a lighter. Quickly, the familiar smell of sage perfumed the air. She seated herself as softly as she could.

I was quiet now, not saying a word. I was still deep in hypnosis, but I knew something was wrong. I was starting to feel a touch of panic rise within me. *Why is she doing this? Sage is for cleansing. What the heck? And what is this gelatinous black blob anyway, and why won't this thing get off me?*

Finally, to my relief, she spoke. However, it wasn't what I expected to hear. "I call now for the divine presence and power of Archangel Michael."

What? An angel? Why the hell is she calling in angels? What good is that going to do? I didn't even believe in angels. I'd assumed archangels were a Christian understanding of what I understood to be Masters or Spirit Guides. Angels were fluffy stuff, and I just wasn't into fluff. Little did I know my belief was about to be altered forever, and this would be the last time I would ever think angels weren't real.

One by one Lorraine called an archangel by name into each of the four corners of the room. As she called out for the second archangel, I noticed a faint orange glow within my inner vision. Up to this point, it had merely been black. By the time she had completed calling in the divine reinforcements, everything in my inner world had changed drastically.

I was completely engulfed in a softly glowing tangerine-colored Light. My entire inner sight was filled with it, until there was nothing else but this Light. I felt tears escaping from under my closed lids. I found myself saturated with a kind of love I had never, ever felt before. Even the birth of my firstborn son could not come close to energy of love that held me now. And it did hold me. It wrapped around me and through me and filled every single cell of my entire being.

Gently and steadily the Light moved into my heart, effortlessly penetrating the protective barricades I had created. Each brick of this wall had been forged from a past full of pain and secured into place by the mortar of "never again." But this Light just kept going.

It moved through and into the brick wall as if it were nothing. It didn't heed the signs that read, "Danger, Keep Out." The Light dissolved all the barriers instantly on contact. It flowed directly into the very core of my tender, wounded heart.

My face was wet and my ears had become a reservoir of tears as I lay there on a worn-in sofa, with a woman I barely knew sitting there watching. This was the last touch of self-awareness I was to have while in the Light. There were no more bull-headed remarks or questions of doubt from me. There was no recollection of me, Cheryl, the individual. My mind had been rendered useless, lost in the most powerful experience of love I have ever known.

I heard nothing and saw no one in this orange Light, yet there was complete communication taking place. It didn't use words or pictures, or anything at all. It was more like a mass of feelings and knowingness that conveyed everything. I understood fully that I was love and that I was deeply loved.

The Light contained a feeling of family, that familiar feeling of deeply knowing someone thoroughly, yet far beyond the ties of human blood. I belonged here. I belonged in this family that was the Light. It was unconditional, caring nothing about any of the things I had ever done. Those things no longer mattered. There was only pure acceptance here. I was loved beyond measure and truly, deeply cared for. It was here that I had purpose. It was here that I had meaning.

This was the feeling I had unknowingly been missing all my life. This is what both called me and eluded me in every moment of my existence. This is what my heart needed, but could never find. And without it, I did not want to live.

Faintly, from somewhere far away, a voice spoke to me, calling out my name. It was as though someone had the volume on low and was slowly turning up the dial.

"Cheryl? Cheryl...what is going on for you?" The words dragged me back into the room, but the Light remained strong within my inner world.

It took a few moments for the electrical pulse to travel from my brain to my lips so I could answer her. My body was so very heavy. My lips felt like enormous weighted rubber flaps.

"I am in Light." My voice sounded as though I was under the influence of heavy tranquilizers and hadn't yet fully awakened. I was far from asleep, however. My ability to perceive everything was crisp and sharp. It was as though my brain had tapped into overdrive. This Light was not simply connecting me to angels or intense love; it was also connecting me to some divine source of knowledge and understanding.

My answer had thrown Lorraine off guard, and questions ensued. She hadn't expected to have her client meander off with the archangels, completely lost in love's abyss.

This flowing orange glow had a strange quality that now owned every ounce of my heart and mind. From within it, I was able to answer any question she asked of me. She asked me a question and I found myself speaking. It was an effortless transference of knowledge and understanding that came through the Light. Taking that information and translating it into words, however, was not so easy. It was instantaneous information. As a question came, the answer was already there waiting. At this point, I was not even sure what she had asked me, but I found myself relaying what the Light was telling me.

I explained to Lorraine that when we experience strong emotions, there is a tendency to tighten certain muscles and slow our breath. Sometimes, if the emotion is strong enough, we'll even hold our breath. The act of stopping the breath slows or even stops the flow of energy created by the emotion. I understood that the energy could be locked or held into that spot and imprinted onto the ethereal energy body, creating an energy pattern that could now be carried into the next life.

10

I can't really say I was impressed or surprised by what was happening in that moment. At this point, I was so deep into hypnosis and the process of what was happening that my thinking mind had almost vanished. The words I spoke all seemed so very natural. The Light, the love, the information—it felt so natural and right. This was how it should be. I didn't question it—nor could I have in my trancelike state.

It was too bad, really. Here I was connected to the greatest source of knowledge and information I had ever known and I couldn't even formulate a question for myself. All I could do was listen to a question and then receive the answer, relaying it to Lorraine. It was probably a good thing. Looking back though, I wished I could have at least asked what my purpose was, why I was here, and how I could be of service. Well, I'm sure I would have also asked something about lottery numbers and what the kids would do with their lives when they grew up. Come to think of it, dwelling within an unlimited source of knowledge, I know I would have gone on quite a roll. It was probably best things happened as they did.

I felt the small tears begin to trickle down the sides of my face once again when I was told it was time to come back. I wanted to stay here. I wanted to remain in this Light. It was like the ultimate paradox—this was where I belonged, yet I couldn't reside here. I didn't want to leave, but I knew I had to. I had unknowingly been waiting for this my whole life and now it was here. It took everything I had to pull away. This beautiful, soft, tangerine-colored Light would be forever imprinted into my memory as one of the single most important experiences of my lifetime. Little did I know that the entire course of my life was about to change, and what I perceived as reality was about to be forever altered.

❦ 2 ❦

Only Crazy People Hear Voices

I sat up slowly. I was still a bit woozy from lying on my back for the last hour and from the overwhelming experience that had just occurred. I rubbed my hands over my thighs and inhaled slowly. I had to take a couple of deep breaths before I felt centered again.

My mind was spinning. I didn't know what to make of this. The Light, the angels, the information, it was all just too much. "So... that was interesting," I said to Lorraine. What an understatement! I couldn't fully believe what had just happened, and I was going to need some time to process it. I am a skeptic by nature, and I needed time to think about it, examine it, and review it before I could make a decision about whether it was real. The old me was back now. My thinking mind was back in full control, no longer squelched by the hypnosis-induced altered state. Even though this had been the single most incredible and powerful event in my life to date, I was still reluctant to believe it. Crazy stuff like that only happened in the books I read, not to me! Maybe I was still in a bit of shock. Whatever it was, I was going to need some time.

Over the next few weeks my dreams were vivid and plentiful.

Slowly, I began to accept the truth about the existence of angels. I could feel their presence with me now throughout the day. I also began meditating at least two hours every day. I had meditated all my life, but had let it fall to the side with the birth of my second child. It was nice to be doing it again, but something about it had subtly changed for me, though the change was vague and hard to pinpoint. Other than the vagueness, everything else seemed perfectly normal, so I tried to ignore the obscure feelings. I just wanted to carry on with life as I always had.

But things were *not* the same. I knew now without a doubt that I was loved very, very much and that I had not been abandoned, as I had believed all these years. I truly reveled in it. I reviewed my experience in the Light and with the angels often because I never, ever wanted to forget what I had felt. I wanted to keep it forever fresh in my memory. And a surprising benefit was that my thoughts of suicide had come to a complete halt. But while I could definitely say my depression had shifted, it had not been removed entirely.

The next big event followed quickly. One day, as usual, I dropped my youngest son off at school. I was anxious to get started with my renewed morning meditation, connecting with my Source. Since he was in his first year of elementary school, he stayed for only half a day. That barely gave me a couple of hours to meditate, shower, clean the house, and get back to the school to pick him up. Meditating came first. If something else did not get done, I didn't care, but there was no way I was going to miss my morning practice for anything. It was only weeks since my life-changing hypnotherapy session and I felt almost addicted to meditation again. I now considered it life support!

My meditation started off like any other meditation. Usually I would sit cross-legged either on the bed or on the floor of my room; that day I was on the bed. I liked meditating in the bedroom, which was small and cozy with just enough room for the bed. I had painted the dark wood-paneled walls a soft buttery yellow. All the trim was white. I had chosen those colors to help me feel more cheerful when I awoke and also to help offset the dark, gloomy days of our west coast winters. I'm sure the colors made a difference for me on some level because I did feel happier in there.

I was struggling a little with swirling thoughts and my "monkey mind" that day, but it settled down quickly, having gotten used to the daily training. I easily found a quietness within me and I rested there within it as I followed my breathing in and out.

If I had been expecting what happened next, it probably wouldn't have alarmed me nearly as much. But I wasn't prepared, and it nearly sent my heart leaping straight out of my chest.

I was following my breath as it moved through my lungs, up my throat, out of my mouth, and then back in and down to complete its cycle. I had been meditating for about fifteen or twenty minutes by now. I decided to focus some attention on my third eye. I wanted to open my inner vision in hopes of actually seeing them, to visually experience these Beings who had planted a seed of love within my heart.

As I brought my attention up to that small space above the middle of my brows, a voice spoke out loud to me. "Focus on the heart," it stated simply.

My body jolted and my arms flailed awkwardly. I'm sure someone would have laughed had they seen my reaction. My eyes shot open while a simultaneous and awkward "ugh" sound escaped from my throat. My heart was palpitating wildly.

Holy shit! I thought. *What was that?* I didn't want to believe that a real voice had just spoken to me, but it appeared that I had no choice because I certainly had not imagined it. I was stunned! *A real voice had just spoken to me!* The sound had come from what seemed like the center of my head. It was as though I had heard it from between my ears, not from outside of my ears.

Utterly shocked, and shaken from my meditation, I wasn't entirely sure what I should do. A part of me wanted to get up and run, but I didn't. For a while, I just sat there dumbly. Was it a good voice or a bad voice? I didn't know. *Is it ever good to hear voices, Cheryl? Was it really a voice? You don't know for sure. Just listen for a minute and see if you hear anything else.* I sat quietly, looking around the room for a few moments, listening and watching. I became concerned that if I had heard something then I might see something too, and I didn't want to see anything, yet I was too frightened to close my eyes. To my relief though, nothing appeared and all was quiet. *It was probably just your imagination.* Yet I knew it wasn't.

I took a couple of deep, slow breaths and closed my eyes again. I let my awareness fall on my heartbeat, which was still strong and quick. I felt my breath flow through my chest and imagined it nourishing my heart with oxygen. It took a couple of minutes, but slowly the palpitations began to fade into a soft rhythmic flow. I simply sat in a crossed-legged position, watching my breath and feeling my heart. I had completely let go of any thoughts of the voice and was back in full flow with my meditation.

Suddenly, the androgynous voice returned. "Breathe from the heart," it instructed. I was slightly startled this time, but not jolted as if lightning had struck me like the first time.

Shit! That was definitely a voice, Cheryl! Oh my freaking God—that was for real this time. Oh my God! Little Miss Skeptical disappeared as the reality of what had just happened sunk in. I knew for certain now that I had heard a voice. I wasn't just crazy. Well, yes, it was crazy to hear voices, but I knew I hadn't imagined it. The audio had definitely come from the center of my own head. I couldn't discern whether it was a good or a bad thing; I just knew I had never experienced anything like that before. A barrage of thoughts appeared all at once and they began an inner dialog with one another.

Oh my God, Cheryl, you are hearing voices. Damn it! They medicate people for this, you know.

Great, just great. I hate those meds. I'm never taking them again! And just when I thought I was actually getting better, I'm turning into a total nutcase? Now I'll be OCD, manic, and schizophrenic—great!

I tried telling myself to just calm down for a few seconds. I wasn't crazy and this wasn't that kind of voice. I had wanted to connect with them and I realized I just had. But it wasn't just the Light this time, as it was in the hypnotherapist's office—it was different. I told myself I was blessed. Yet another part of me thought that most people wouldn't call this a blessing—they'd call it lunacy. How could I tell anyone? I could just imagine the cynical response: "Oh yes, the Voice told her to do it."

I changed my mind and decided I needed to tell Brent. *He's your husband, Cheryl—he's not going to think you're a lunatic. Since crazy people don't actually know they're crazy, he'll be able to tell you if you're crazy or not. You have to tell him.*

Eventually, I managed to stop the panic and pull myself together. The voice had asked me to breathe from my heart. *Do it Cheryl. Just trust. It's okay. Do the breathing.* I corralled my thoughts and got focused on the task at hand. It took several minutes to get my breathing and heart rate back to something near normal. I had to settle the jitters and anxiety first.

Once I was calm enough, I settled in for another round of breathing. I wasn't completely sure of what I was doing; I just tried to do what felt natural, as if I were actually breathing from my heart. I imagined my heart was where the air entered and exited my body. Not one drop of oxygen could enter my body until it passed through my heart first. I visualized each molecule of air being reinforced with love energy before it was allowed to pass into my system. From there, it flowed freely and nurtured every cell within my being.

Each exhaled breath still carried the vibration of love, and it emanated from me in large waves and surrounded me. As I continued the rhythmic love flow of breath, it all felt very natural. An unexpected result, however, was the sensation that my heart was expanding in size. I didn't realize it at the time, but I was energetically opening my heart-center in a very powerful way. I surprised myself at how easily I was able to follow the instructions to breathe from the heart without fully knowing what to do. And the sensation from doing the heart breathing was exhilarating to me; I became much more tuned into different energies.

This experience fueled my passion for my morning ritual of connecting with Source. My bedroom became the classroom and I eagerly attended class each day. My instructors were of another place, teaching me the basics of energy and intuition. Sometimes, with words, they would convey the lesson of the day. Other times they would communicate through an understanding or knowing, which would often be accompanied by symbols and/or feelings.

I also felt more guided outside of the meditations. For example, I would come across reading material that related to what I was being taught. This was especially true of the inner-vision part of the studies, where I was learning that seeing intuitively is just like using the imagination. As a matter of fact, they originated from the same faculty. My spirit teachers guided me to the teachings of Thoth, who was an ancient Egyptian deity. Even though I had never had any interest in Egyptian teachings, I knew I needed to read this little booklet. It contained just one paragraph where Thoth spoke of the importance of developing the imagination as a part of intuition. Everything just clicked when I read that. I understood. Within just a couple of weeks, my inner visions were flowing in full. Now, not only did I have audio contact, but I had visual contact as well. This really helped to move my teachings along.

After a very short time, my meditation routine had altered completely. Under my teachers' watchful eyes and loving guidance, my education continued. The biggest change in my daily meditation was the method I now used to connect with them.

I would start off by grounding my energy. I'd visualize the energy flowing out and down from my tailbone and into the core of the Earth. From there it would spread and grow, looking very much like the roots of a tree. This process was important, and I didn't rush it; I waited until I could feel a magnetic pull from the Earth. Only then would I move on.

Next, I would see and feel a beautiful surge of energy from Mother Earth that would travel up from the Earth's core and into my newly laid roots. The energy would pulse and spin and glow as it traveled slowly up the roots, where it would enter my body through my spine. Once inside me, the energy would spread down through my legs and into every organ as it made its way up each vertebra until it reached my heart. The energy would then flow into my heart.

From there, the emotion of love would surge through me. My heart chakra would respond by expanding and emanating love. I would watch this energy grow until it became large enough to fill my entire body. Then it would reach out farther, filling every bit of space within the room. Ever growing and expanding, my heart energy would engulf the entire planet. I would hold the Earth with my heart energy and I would give my gratitude to Mother Earth and everyone on it. And when I said it, I meant it. A physiological reaction occurred, as often a tear or two would fall from my eyes. I was feeling the world deeply on an energetic level and it was beautiful.

Next, the energy would continue up my back and into my neck. I'd often see it activating each chakra on its way to my crown. From there, in an outward spiraling motion, it would flow upward through the ceiling, the roof, past the sky, reaching out into the vastness of the universe. Ultimately, it would reach the heavens—the dimension or space where Souls exist when not incarnated. I would see and feel my energy spreading out again, like a tree's branches, only now they were grounding me to ethereal worlds.

Then, just as it flowed from the Earth, the energy of the Heavens would flow down through the universe, through the roof, and into my room until it entered my crown. It flowed onward to my heart and then eventually back into the ground of the Earth, into my roots. With my grounding complete, my attention would fall on my breath, and I would begin the heart breathing that I had been taught on the first day the voices spoke to me.

I was reassured that these steps were vitally important. They served a multitude of uses at one time. Moving all the energy through the heart-center in love and gratitude helped to anchor the physical energy of the body. It assisted the body in functioning smoothly while enabling the energy bodies to function at a much higher vibration. It facilitated my spiritual evolution and growth in learning to operate more closely as my Higher Self. At the same time, it switched the tracks that my thoughts normally used. Instead of thinking and operating from my head, it would be channeled through the heart-mind instead. Stated in a more simple way, the main operation of thinking would be conducted through the higher mind or heart-mind, rather than the lower mind—the ego. When I ran my energy through my heart and I worked in these higher frequencies, an energy field was created that could more easily connect into Source energy because it more closely matched Source energy. My spirit teachers explained that grounding with the heavens also helped to facilitate our communication.

One thing in particular was stated over and over again: I was to learn how to function from the heart-mind. This level of functioning carried the highest possible vibration and would quickly move me into the alignment where I needed to be in order to do my work. What I understood was that this is a vital part of our ascension process, our evolution as Souls. I'm not talking about 2012 here. Not once was this date mentioned or anything even remotely close to the "end of days." I am talking about the natural order of evolution and progress. We are made to evolve, and we will, each in our own time. We can either slow this process or assist in developing it. Operating from the heart-mind will greatly aid this process.

It should be mentioned that at this time, absolutely no one

spoke of the heart or functioning from the heart. As a matter of fact, when I shared this with any of my friends during these early years, they would continually advise me to focus on my third eye and crown if I wanted to develop my intuition. But I now knew better.

My new teachers shared with me that the most effective way to facilitate intuitive connections was through the heart-center. Develop the heart and the rest would follow. Every single thing I did or was asked to do was always from the heart-center. My teachers told me this must become my main mode of operating, and I never questioned them. When I thought about it, who was I really going to listen to? Was I going to take the advice of girlfriends who had learned everything they knew from the books they read? Or was I going to listen to the voice of Spirit that spoke directly inside of my own head and directly to my heart? It wasn't a difficult choice.

My husband had taken it all very well. What a sport he was—he genuinely encouraged my communication with my spirit teachers. He had always been my biggest supporter. Brent trained standardbred racehorses for a wealthy millionaire, and we lived on his sixty-acre farm, which boarded up to one hundred and sixty head of horses at any given time. Each day when Brent arrived home from work, he would ask for the daily update.

There were times when the things they said to me were so far out there that I had a very hard time understanding, let alone believing in them. Brent, my champion, would simply listen without judgment. Usually he would break into a large smile as the daily report came to a close.

This was one of the most difficult times in my spiritual growth, mainly because my inner skeptic had a tough time taking in what was happening. I am not a blind follower of anything; I don't just believe in things for the sake of believing. I have a very logical mind. And even though I was having a direct experience with these new teachers, they were talking directly to me, showing me, teaching me—I still had a hard time with it.

I also was plagued with doubt. I continued to doubt what I saw or that I had understood it correctly. I doubted everything.

When I was very young, my father was obsessed with ESP and the powers of the mind. Anything to do with psychic abilities, hypnosis, telekinesis, prediction, and speaking to those who have passed away utterly fascinated him. He was also obsessed with UFOs and extraterrestrials. A Sunday did not go by when we didn't watch his favorite show, which was all about the world's mysteries, UFO sightings, unexplained phenomena, and contact from beyond the grave. That show used to frighten me terribly at times, but I couldn't pull my eyes away from it.

Thanks to shows like that and *The Amazing Kreskin*, my father often used my two sisters, my brother, and me as his guinea pigs. And I was unusually good at most tasks he gave me: guess the card color, which hand is it in, what cup is it under, what shape am I thinking, sensing spirits, feeling for energy and cold spots. The list goes on and on. I could do all of those little tricks with ease. Most of the time I stood out from my siblings, which I didn't enjoy. Even worse was when my father's friends would come over and I had to perform the tricks for them. By my very nature, since birth, I have never been comfortable being the center of attention. A small degree of it was nice, to be seen and acknowledged, but this was more like being under a huge spotlight with me on center stage. I didn't like it one bit. So I began to stuff my intuition away.

Well, I thought I had, anyway. I stuffed those things as far away as I could. That still didn't stop strange, silent people from making an occasional appearance in my room at night; nor did it prevent the creeped-out feelings I would get in certain places. I always knew the state of someone else's energy, but that ability helped to ensure my own safety, so I kept it in the toolbox. When you grow up in chaos, the ability to detect others' energy is a good tool to have.

So although I wasn't able to stifle my intuition completely, I was able to consciously block out much of it. In doing so, I had actually stuffed away many of the natural gifts I was born with and was meant to use during my lifetime. I now believe this was a large contributing factor to my depression. I had incredible gifts I was meant to share with others. But I had tossed them aside, squelched them, and left them to rot so I didn't have to deal with the uncomfortable feelings of being noticed. If anyone ever mentioned being intuitive or psychic, I was the first one to say "Not me!" And I fully believed it. I had completely convinced myself that I hadn't one ounce of intuition in me.

I wasn't yet entirely sure what the sum of the after-effects of the tangerine Light was, but I did know one thing. Like it or not, the Light had blown my intuition open to how God intended it to be. And I wasn't sure if I did like it. It was going to take some getting used to. The fact that I pooh-poohed a lot of stuff and doubted everything all the time didn't help the situation much. Thank God that Brent, my rock, was there to help me through it. Things were only going to get weirder from this point on.

3

Taking Out the Trash

Life had taken an incredible turn; however, the depression still had its hold on me. The only difference now was that I knew I belonged here. The Light had given me that. I knew I had a place on this planet and I was loved beyond measure. At least now I had a solid footing. I wasn't just wailing around helplessly in the blackness anymore.

I knew a major part in my battle with depression was going to be my thinking. Since my passion had always been psychology and the human mind, I learned as much as I could about these subjects. I came across some very interesting research studies. Scientists had discovered that the neural pathways of people who suffered from depression were greatly reduced compared with happy, healthy people. They found that a regular person's brain uses a wide variety of pathways that are in balance over the entire brain region. In contrast, those with depression create what could be compared to a couple of rabbit trails, meaning the majority of their thoughts use the same small number of selected neural pathways over and over.

People suffering from depression do not use the whole region of the brain with any regularity.

If I were to follow this reasoning, obviously, two things had to happen. One, I had to get my mind to start building new neural pathways, and lots of them. Two, I had to stop the transmission of thoughts from taking the rabbit trails. I was going to have to create detour signs and offer my thoughts alternative routes. Stated simply, I had to change my thinking.

Each night before I went to sleep, I would lie in bed and try to think of something I had never seen or thought of before. I'd imagine a new type of insect that had not yet been discovered. I'd create a new type of flower no one had ever seen before, my mind shaping its petals and choosing its colors. Or I would imagine I had another child, a little girl. Then I would allow her personality to take shape, her physical features to appear, and so on. Whatever I could come up with to think of something absolutely new and different, that's where I'd let my thoughts flow. It was the only way I could think of to begin building new neural pathways for my thoughts to travel on.

I also knew I was using learned responses to situations, events, and everyday occurrences that were keeping me stuck on the rabbit trail. This part was really hard. It took a very concentrated and committed effort to monitor my thoughts as much as possible throughout the day. I was going to have to recreate my natural responses to things. When I caught a thought that was going down the trail, I would first acknowledge it. I would look at it fully, trying to trace its roots and origins. The more insight, understanding, perspective, and knowledge I had of my own thoughts and beliefs, the more I was empowered to do something about them.

But watching thoughts is like watching clouds. They are always moving and shifting and changing right before your eyes. Trying to find the source of a thought is just like trying to find the source of a cloud. A cloud doesn't originate in the sky, where you found it. It originates from below, from the pools of water on the earth. It might have been one or many different pools of water that contributed evaporated molecules to that cloud.

Thoughts are the same. The source comes from below, in the pools of the conscious, subconscious, and unknown vast cerebral territory. Even though tracing the origins of a thought back to its absolute source is extremely difficult, if you take some time to thoroughly assess the thought—the quality, the feelings it creates, and the beliefs it contains—then you can get a pretty good idea of its source.

If you had a cloud that was releasing polluted, chemical-filled acid raindrops, the only way to clean the cloud would be to clean the water from where it came. This is true of our thoughts as well. And was it ever raining a bunch of polluted garbage in my world, from a stream of thought clouds that only traveled on a few narrow paths through my inner sky. In order to clean things up, I was going to have to use the tools and equipment I had in a very diligent and dedicated manner.

After my last suicide attempt, which was now over ten years ago, a friend of mine had invited me to do a weekend workshop. It was a psychology-based transpersonal and spiritual workshop. It was there that I met my husband, and I ended up staying in this spiritual community for about six months. My teacher, P.T. Mistlberger, was not a pansy when it came to personal growth work. He had studied with some of the greatest teachers on the planet, and he had a way of looking directly through a person's mind and calling bullshit when he saw it. In P.T.'s own words, "Everything we deal with on the journey to awakening is psychological resistance to uncovering truth, and in the process, uncovering our almost endless capacity for self-deception and the avoidance of truth." This was decidedly not a course for the meek of heart. There were times I felt I was much too meek for this kind of deep introspection and ego busting.

Everything I said, did, and did not do was up for evaluation.

With my ego under constant watch, I was gaining enormous insights. I was getting called out on all of my beliefs, thoughts and actions. What I learned about myself, the shadow, and the ego had given me a set of tools that became invaluable. With what I had learned from P.T., I became fully equipped to take on the monumental task of becoming my own Master.

I used what I had learned back then and I looked at every conscious thought I could catch. I examined it, tracing it back as best I could to its source. I examined the beliefs it carried, where those beliefs had come from, and why I had them. I allowed myself to really feel the energy they carried and the emotion they created. I looked at them all, even my most dark and ugly thoughts—especially those ones. Few thoughts were denied inspection. Few were buried or sent back to be hidden away again. I looked at every thought I could catch, without judgment. They were neither good nor bad, they just *were*. There was a saying I used to keep me going when this got tough: "To know your own darkness is to know your own Light. For without the darkness there can be no Light."

This was a slow process and it certainly wasn't an instant cure. It actually took years of doing this faithfully. It was the only way to eliminate the rabbit trails and clean my inner world out. Today I do not have depressive thoughts and I do not suffer from depression at all. My reactions to things are much different now. I still get sad. I still get down. Things still suck. But I don't get carried into the black void. I still want to get out of bed, even when things are going wrong. My head doesn't tell me I don't deserve to be alive. My heart doesn't ache in pain at the thought of having to go through one more day of hell on Earth. Things have definitely come a long way.

Doing shadow and ego work isn't easy. These certainly were not my favorite place to delve into. Within the spiritual or new age community, for a very long time there has been a belief that we should only think good thoughts or we shouldn't dwell on anything perceived as negative. But I knew I couldn't just banish these thoughts and beliefs that lingered within me. Where was I going to banish them to? The ethereal? I knew full well that even if I tried not to acknowledge this part of myself, it wouldn't just disappear. Where could these negative thoughts possibly go if I simply ignored or denied them?

I completely understood the premise for this long-held spiritual belief of holding only positive thoughts: that we are what we think, that what we think and feel is what we will get back, that the vibrations of those kinds of thoughts are lower and we all want vibrations of a higher level, that we all want to manifest only good things so we can think and say only good things. But to me—and this may sound harsh—the entire groundwork or basis of these teachings has been warped and mutilated into a devastating and self-destructive misconception. It's been taken out of its true context and twisted. It actually mirrors the concepts of religious conformity. It is controlling and carries with it a hint of "sin." *If you don't think good thoughts, then you aren't good. You'll pay, you know. You'll have bad energy and will manifest bad things. It will mean you aren't a loving person and you are of a lower vibration.*

There is only *one* way to get to a place of true positiveness and that is through our own darkness. We are born from the darkness of the womb into the Light. We fade into darkness when we die, then go to the Light. And in order for any of us to access our true Light, we too must pass through our own darkness. It is the only way.

It can be compared to the trash we accumulate each week in our homes. If you were to deny the existence of your trash, even though it accumulated daily, your home would be overrun with garbage. The stench would repel any visitor to your home, you would have nowhere clean to sleep or eat, and you would be living in utter filth, which manifests into disease. Or if you were to just take the garbage and stuff it away in your garage day after day, it wouldn't be long before your garage was too full to hold it. It would cascade out of the door every time you opened it to throw another bag in. Then you would have to toss the bags onto your lawn or out your back door. Eventually, you would be overrun with filth.

The same principle applies when we deny or suppress our negative thoughts and beliefs. They aren't going anywhere. All that mind garbage is still there, even if you choose to turn a blind eye to it. It is there and it does stink. It just builds and builds, accumulating until there is no more room to hold it. Soon you find yourself overrun with it and it affects your daily living. You might feel a low-grade anger or resentment. You might find yourself using addictive behavior to distract you from your inner trash—overeating or keeping an overly busy schedule or spending too much time at your computer or even in meditation or prayer—just so you don't have to face it. It can also show up as a form of depression or general malaise or unhappiness. You just don't feel good inside. You try and try to be happy, but somehow that happiness eludes you. Things never seem to go as planned.

The worst part is that much of this behavior is highly unconscious. It's vague and hard to put a finger on exactly. So instead of being a super-positive, high-vibrating being, you are actually emanating a barrage of hidden negative energy. And your ego? Well, all the while your ego is going to tell you that you are doing the right thing, that the trash doesn't exist, and if someone or something does point or hint at your hidden trash, you will find yourself triggered and defensive. That is the biggest clue.

In order to truly reach that place of high vibration and positive energy, we must all deal with the trash. Every single one of us creates trash, has residual trash, hides trash, and reeks of trash, each in our own personal way. We must acknowledge our negative thoughts, our ugly beliefs, our most deeply intimate, private, and secret stuff we think we must keep hidden from the world. We need to examine it, expose it, analyze it, and accept it. Then, only through the spark of forgiveness and the fire of love—true self-love and acceptance—will the dark be transformed into Light. Only then will your energy be authentic, pure, and positive. It's similar to taking your trash to an incinerator. The flames of the fire transform the trash. And within yourself, the flames of self-love and acceptance transform your shadow and darkness.

We have all come to this temporal world to be incarnated, to be human. We have chosen to be human and to experience the feelings and emotions that only humans have. Therefore, it is vital to accept our humanness. *All* of our humanness. We have not come here to ascend around or over our human selves. We have come here to ascend and evolve *through* our human selves.

I discovered that everything breaks down to love. Everything. I had to love myself and love my humanness. I had to love my Light and love my dark. I learned that to deny or reject even one part of me was an act of *un-love*, and I was denying my own Light.

Even though I hadn't intended it, that is exactly what I had been doing. I'd been denying my shadow and denying my Light. Yet I knew better—I had supposedly learned this ten years earlier! It's not that I was all fluff and bubbles, only wanting to talk love and Light—anyone who knew me could tell you I was far from that. What I suffered from was spiritual ignorance. Who likes to linger inside their own darkness? Not me, so my ego had found a way to fool me into thinking I didn't have to. My ego had me believing I'd already learned this stuff and had already done more than enough work on it, and that was good enough. As long I just kind of skirted around the outsides, doing just enough to keep me sane, then I was "doing the work." But I hadn't been doing the work, at least not on a deep enough level to produce a lasting effect and positive change. Unknowingly, I had fallen for the lie, and I wasn't doing the work in any sort of way that kept my ego in check. In the meantime, my trash had built up. I had some hard work ahead of me.

Along with my new trailblazing, cloud-busting, and trash-incinerating commitments, I also made sure I consumed three to four tablespoons of mixed omega oils daily. Omegas literally feed and nourish the brain. The typical Western diet is severely lacking in these essential oils. Through my research, I learned that a lack of omegas in the diet was directly linked to anxiety and panic attacks, postpartum and chronic depression, hormone imbalances such as premenstrual syndrome, Alzheimer's disease, bipolar disorder, and even attention deficit disorder. I suffered from all those maladies, minus the Alzheimer's. So I knew it was vital. I tried to take the most holistic approach possible, covering every aspect I could think of. Combining this with the thought repatterning, the daily mediation, and opening my heart-center in love and gratitude, I was well on my way to healing.

The training with my teachers continued as well. At the time we began covering some basics of energy work, "coincidentally," my younger son developed a nasty little patch of psoriasis on his elbow. It drove him to distraction, as it was constantly itchy. I decided to take some of my new energy training and put it to work. Sure enough, within just a couple of days the patch was nearly invisible, so I stopped working on it. I was highly skeptical that anything I had done was actually a part of the healing. Within a week, it returned, and again, although I doubted my healing was making any difference, I worked on it. Just as before, within a couple of days it was gone. Still, I was not convinced I had anything to do with the healing.

I'm not sure why I am so skeptical and stubborn; it's just the way I am and I can't help it. My husband, however, was completely convinced the first time around that I had a talent for healing.

"Cheryl, how could you not believe you had anything to do with this?" Brent asked one afternoon when he had stopped in for lunch.

"Come on. I have a strange experience in an orange light with angels and now I can talk to Spirit Guides—that's hard enough to take. Now you're thinking I've become a healer too? Give me a break!"

He wasn't going to give me a break, however. He knew many

of my self-doubts were stemming from years of believing I was nothing and had nothing to offer. To ask me to accept that I now actually had gifts was a complete one-hundred-and-eighty-degree turnaround. This was going to take some time to accept.

But Brent, being the clever guy he was, had come up with a plan. An experiment, actually. He sat across the kitchen table, grinning as he always did when he knew he had one up on me.

"What?" I asked in a half-annoyed tone. I knew that smile well and I knew he was up to something.

"I know how to settle this once and for all." He smiled even more broadly now.

"Oh really? And how is that? How in the world do you plan to prove I'm the one making a difference with the psoriasis?"

"Well," he said, spooning another large swallow of soup into his mouth, "the vet came by today and diagnosed two horses with the same injury. They both have torn suspensories in nearly the same spots on their legs. And I was thinking you should work on one of the horses. The other one we'll leave to heal naturally, the way we always do. If you're making a difference, we'll be able to see it."

"Huh?" I was a little nervous about this proposition. Yes, it was a really good idea, but what if I agreed to do it and there was no difference in the horse? Then what would I be left with, other than the knowledge that I really didn't have a gift for healing? I was half afraid of the answer. Worse still, what if I *did* make a difference? Then what? Then I would have to let go of these deep-rooted beliefs that I had nothing to offer the world. My ego was in a quandary with this one. I would then have to accept my gift and the responsibility that went along with it. "What's a torn suspensory?" I asked.

Brent went on to explain that the suspensory ligament was like an elastic band just below the horse's knee. It was similar to a bungee cord. However, when it was overstretched, the elastics of the band would break, leaving a hole in the ligament. The problem with this type of injury was that it usually took six to eight months to heal and it almost always ended a horse's career.

"How big is this hole?"

"Oh, they're big. They're about the size of two pencil erasers put together," he said, his eyebrows raised.

Was he really shocked about something that sounded like a teeny-weeny hole? "That's it? A couple of pencil erasers? Come on now, is this a serious injury or are you just trying to humor me?" Now I was really annoyed.

"No Cheryl, I'm not. They really are big as far as suspensory injuries go. The holes are usually half that size!" He paused and tilted his head to the side. "You can do this. Have a little faith in yourself...because I have faith in you."

Oh, he had me with that one, and I remained quiet. He was right. God, I hated it when he was right. The worst that could happen is the horse would receive some loving, healing energy. Whether it ultimately helped to heal him was another matter all together.

Now that I had a job to do, my training really kicked into gear. I didn't know how to connect to the horse. I was in my bedroom meditating and the horse was out in a paddock on our farm. This is when the knowledge that there is absolutely no time, distance, or space between living forms really solidified for me. I had read about this before and I believed it, but now it became a concept with experiential meaning and I understood it fully.

Most of the information transferred from my teachers was coming through a wordless explanation; as if by osmosis, my mind absorbed the teachings. The main form of conveyance was through images, symbols, feelings, and strangely, information that just seemed to somehow appear in my head. Only occasionally did they use audible words to communicate with me. Oh, but how I loved it when they did! I was no longer frightened by them.

I needed to make an energetic connection with my new case study, Lance. Following my teachers' instructions, I simply repeated his name gently in mind until I could feel the connection. They had previously explained that the intention alone to connect was enough for it to happen. The energy of intention was very powerful and was the groundwork for anything I did. Before doing anything, I was to always clarify my intentions—what it was I wanted to do and why I wanted to do it. From there things would just flow. I learned some of the healing techniques through trial and error, and others through direct guidance.

With Lance, I could actually see the horse, but everything was blue outlines on a black background. I could see where the injury was and how it looked, and I could monitor the energy as it entered and worked its magic. Not surprisingly, one of the keys in doing good energy work was that I always had to be centered in my heart before I began. Also, all the energy that I moved was to run through my heart first.

A few days after beginning the healing, Lance, my new equine friend, began to "talk" to me. I didn't hear his voice, but I understood everything he needed to convey to me. I understood he had suffered emotional trauma. He pointed at experiences he'd had with a previous trainer that had broken his spirit. He had no desire to race and would rather be injured and in pain than go through that experience again. So now I wasn't just going to work on healing a physical injury, I was going to have to work on his heart and spirit as well. Again, right when I needed them, my teachers were there, guiding me through the process.

To make a long story short, Brent had the vet scan Lance's leg only two months after I started working with him. Earlier that morning, Lance had told me he was healed. Still, I doubted what I received. I would definitely need a confirmation.

The vet took one look at the scan and her mouth dropped open. "Oh my goodness! It's pretty much healed! Brent, what did you use on him? Whatever it is, you'd better bottle it because you're going to make a fortune from it. I've never seen a suspensory ligament heal like this in my entire career as a vet. And that's no understatement!" She was absolutely dumbfounded.

Brent had a good secret chuckle over her response. There was no way he was going to tell her his wife had sat on the bedroom floor for the last two months, talking with both the horse and her Spirit Guides, while she sent injured Lance healing energy.

Brent then had the vet scan the control subject, the other horse with the same injury that I had not worked on. As expected, there was no change to her injury whatsoever.

Eventually, the vet did break Brent's vow of silence. There was no way she was going to let him walk around with one of the greatest healing secrets she had ever seen without knowing what it was. She became even more insistent when, not more than a couple months later, the control horse was also healed. I just couldn't let the little mare suffer when I now knew I could help her. Once the vet saw the healing of the second horse, she was determined to extract the miracle cure from Brent.

She took the news of my healing abilities quite well, but she was thoroughly disappointed that the cure wasn't a marketable product after all. However, she did have me work on her own horses and many of her clients' as well. I didn't only do healing work; I also did equine psychology. I found that most horses were very eager to have someone listen to them, and many of them were quick to reveal their owners' mistreatment.

I always found it difficult to report my findings to owners during my intuitive visits with their horses. I had to work daily to remove my ego from the picture. I had a deep fear of being wrong—or judged. I was afraid that what I might say would not be the right thing, or that what I had seen was not accurate. That was where faith came in. I had to trust myself, Spirit, and the entire intuitive process. If I heard it or saw it, I had to say it. I couldn't allow my personal stuff to get in the way of doing God's work. This was a great learning curve for me.

Word about my unique talent spread. I helped quite a number of horses and a few dogs, but I helped even more owners to become better owners. I even worked—long distance—on horses for a trainer in Australia, and he witnessed a great improvement in his horses. I would tell him what they needed, wanted, or didn't want, and he always followed through on what I told him. If they needed healing, I always did what I could. He was so impressed that he wanted to meet me and have me visit his horses personally. He paid in full for my return ticket to Australia. Needless to say, I was more than happy to fulfill his request!

4

Alternate Realities Can Be Very Sneaky

I was beginning to be in a much more trusting place with myself as far as accepting the intuitive information I received, and I was now able to accept my intuition as a part of my life. This brought me tremendous healing. I was finally embracing the gifts I had been given, which I had denied for so long. Looking back on my life with my newfound perspective, I realized I always had a deep intuitive connection with Spirit. Just because I had consciously denied it did not mean it wasn't there or I didn't feel it. My spirituality had been the only tether of hope I had to cling to most days when I felt I had nothing else to live for.

I realize now that much of what the doctors had defined as obsessive–compulsive disorder was me acting on the intuitive information I was receiving. Most of what I received then, and still do today, comes in the form of *knowing.* It just appears there; I can't explain it any better than that. But I feel these knowings from within my core, from my heart. They are not just thoughts in my head. And to not follow these knowings or to go against them fills me with a strange sense of dread, a vague feeling I am doing something wrong. Of course, there was no logic to a lot of what I chose to do. It wasn't for the logical mind to understand. I followed my heart in what I was guided to do. Amazingly, no matter what I did or what situation I found myself in, I was always completely taken care of. If my heart felt the calling, then I did it, and no one could talk me out of something once I felt it in my heart.

I love how messages from Spirit can come to us through the mouths of others. I received one of those messages during a phone call with my mom. We were reminiscing about the past and laughing about some of the wild things I'd done when she said to me, "Cher, you've always done really strange things I could never understand, but things seem to always work out well for you. It's like God always takes care of you." I immediately felt that familiar rush of warmth in my chest and throat, and I knew tears were soon to follow. That one tiny statement meant so very much to me. My mother never talked like that or about God for that matter, but she really meant this. And deep down, I knew it was true. I was taken care of. I had never really been abandoned.

My entire world was changing from what it once had been. My heart was truly open now, and I was ready to give and receive whatever came my way. The fact that my ten-year wedding anniversary was here was another great reminder of just how far I'd come. Even though we had not had a legal ceremony, it was a real ceremony and I had pledged to walk the path of personal and spiritual awareness with my partner in life. I had a lot of gratitude for my husband and I wanted to show him how much.

The day of our anniversary, I had spent the afternoon on the phone calling tattoo shops. That morning, it had popped into my head that I should set up an appointment for us to get matching tattoos. I loved surprises and I loved surprising people, and Brent was about to get a big one! We touched on the topic once before, so I figured that was enough to make the decision. I'd found the most beautiful Celtic knot heart I had ever seen. I was so excited.

As I prepared everything for the evening ahead, I was joyous and excited. It felt as though I had just started dating Brent again. My heart was bursting with love for this incredible man who had stood by me throughout all these tumultuous years.

We enjoyed a quiet dinner at our favorite restaurant, and all the while I was giggling and smirking. He knew I was up to something. As we walked back to the car, I told him to go over to the passenger's side as I would be driving now.

"Where are we going?" he asked, looking at me with leery eyes.

"It's a surprise!" I blurted out. I was too excited to talk slowly. "And you are gonna *love* it!"

His eyes narrowed to a squint, his face blank as he looked at me. "You know I don't like surprises."

I laughed in response. "Oh, but you're going to like this one, big boy—don't you worry!" And I started to giggle even harder. He just rolled his eyes and went back to watching the road.

As I neared the parking lot to our final destination, he was now hunching to get a better look out the window. I wished he hadn't done that!

"What the hell!" he exclaimed. "A tattoo parlor, Cheryl? Really?"

"Yes!" I answered, maintaining my upbeat energy. He could be such a party pooper sometimes, but I knew how to handle him. I just had to be happy about it and soon he'd feel the same.

I opened the car door and stepped out. I noticed, though, that I did not hear the sound of his door opening. I bent down to look inside at him. "Well, aren't you coming?" I asked, trying to sound surprised by his lack of enthusiasm.

"Cheryl, I don't want a tattoo," he said. He was serious. He actually sounded a little scared, probably because he was a wimp when it came to pain, and also because he knew I almost always got my way and he wasn't going to make it out of this one unmarked.

"Oh hon..." I sighed, trying to sound sympathetic. I closed my door and walked around to the other side. He just sat there looking out at me. Yes, it was definitely time for me to take action.

I opened the door and sat down on his lap. I wrapped my arms around his neck and kissed him gently on the cheek. Judging by the stiffness of his movements, I could tell the guy was genuinely frightened. Now, maybe you could call it manipulation, if you really wanted to look at it that way. I saw it differently, however. I was just going to help him understand he did actually indeed want this.

I told him about the tattoo I had chosen for us. I knew how much he loved knot work. I explained to him what the symbol meant to me and how much I loved him. I told him every reason why I loved him and how very special he was to me in my life. I meant every word I said. He was the greatest man I had ever known. He was my soul mate, my partner, my lover, and my best friend. The tears trickled down my cheeks. My heart was open and full of love. I kissed him again.

"All right," he sighed. "Let's go. But you get yours first and I'll watch. Then I'll decide if I'm going to get one too."

"Really?" I asked. I sounded surprised, but I wasn't. I had known all along he would.

Happily, the two of us made our way into the tattoo shop. Well, I was happy anyway. I had to smile. No matter what, Brent was always a good sport.

Since I was going first, Brent stood at a distance, but still close enough to watch. We had been escorted into a small room. Equipment was jammed everywhere, and sample tattoos adorned the walls. The place was a bit of a dive, I had to admit.

I was getting my tattoo on my lower back, so the artist had me straddle a chair with its backrest to my chest. It was only a foot away from the wall. My face nearly touched the brochures and papers that hung from the corkboard. My back was facing out to the room.

As the artist began to prepare the equipment, she realized she needed more supplies, which were stored in the room beside us. I continued to read the wall, filled with anticipation.

And then, suddenly, it happened. To be honest, I'm not even sure how it happened. One moment I was reading a brochure and the next moment the wall was gone. But not just the wall—the whole world as I knew it had vanished. The solid mass which had housed the room had disintegrated. Now I was looking out into a vastness. If I had to put a measurement to it, I would say I was seeing out into the distance for hundreds of miles.

This was unlike anything I had ever seen or experienced before. It was filled with pastel-like colors that were extremely difficult to describe. The air, if that is what it was, was a soft shade of baby pink. There was no land and no sky, just a vast openness of soft baby-pink air. The feeling, the colors—it was all very soothing, almost hypnotic. Within my vision, floating through the air, were three large bubbles. They looked almost like the kind of bubbles we would blow as children, using dish detergent, but much bigger. They were translucent, shimmering with pastel colors that reflected and refracted like rainbows in a crystal.

It wasn't so much how the three bubbles looked, which was astonishing in itself, but how they moved—very distinctly and with purpose, soothing and calming. It was as though they were alive and not inanimate objects at all. I was completely mesmerized by these floating iridescent circles and how they slowly danced through the air.

I'm not sure how long I sat looking into this world, but it seemed as though I had been watching for a very long time. All of a sudden, I remembered me. I remembered I was Cheryl and I had been sitting in a tattoo parlor, staring at a wall. *Oh my God—I'm lost in some other world. How am I ever going to get back?*

I felt a wave of fear rush through my body, and I think this is when I became aware I was talking out loud.

I heard Brent's panicked voice behind me, but in my vision all I could see was this perfectly pink and pastel world. That sent an even bigger wave of fear rushing through me. This was a new feeling—I truly didn't know if I was going to make it back to the world I belonged in.

"My eyes! My eyes!" I found myself repeating. "Oh my God, Brent, oh my God! My eyes!" The vision held strong as a huge new crescendo of fear now overtook me. Then, just as suddenly as it came, it began to vanish. I literally watched the molecules of the wall and paper reappearing, the beautiful pastel world disappearing behind it. Only when it had vanished completely did I have full control of my body once more.

I turned to Brent, panic stricken. And when I saw the look of pure terror on his face, it only elevated mine more. "Oh my God, hon...oh my *God!*" These were the only words I could extract from my vocabulary that could possibly describe how I felt.

"What is *wrong?*" he wailed at me. Concern, fear, and disbelief all wrestled their way from his voice.

"I don't know! One minute I was sitting here and the next minute I was gone."

"No, you weren't! You were right here the whole time."

I only had a few moments to explain myself to Brent before the artist returned with her ink. After she did, I said nothing more of the strange other dimension that had opened itself to me. I surely was not going to speak about that in front of a stranger. This was the very thing they medicated people for! *Oh, my Lord, Cheryl. What is happening to you?*

Brent did end up getting the tattoo as well, though he was barely able to take the pain of it. But our new skin art was not the topic of discussion as we made our way back home. Brent had no clue what had really happened back at the shop, and now he wanted every detail. Neither of us knew what the pastel world was or why it happened. We could only agree that it was indeed one of the strangest events to date.

The next morning, it was all I could do to keep my impatience at bay. Now that Jaden, my youngest child, attended first grade for the entire day, he rode the bus to school. I stared down our rolling country road, eagerly waiting for the first glimpse of orange to appear over the hill. I was nearly jumping up and down when the bus finally arrived. I hurriedly kissed my little guy goodbye and ran all the way back down our farm's long driveway. The horses in the paddock beside me must have tuned in to my excitement because they decided it was a good idea to trot along the fence beside me. I loved watching the big puffs of steam billow from their noses as they snorted with contagious excitement.

I flung my shoes off my feet and hustled across the house. All I wanted to do was get myself settled on the bedroom floor. I had no idea what really happened the night before, but I did know several Spirits who did! I had reviewed the experience with Brent a couple of times from start to finish on our drive home last night. Of course, he had absolutely no clue what it was I had seen or how it had happened. I thought I had a bit of an idea, but it was only a theory at this point. I thought I had "broken through the veil," so to speak. It was possible that my consciousness had somehow spontaneously shifted into a different plane of reality. I also theorized that the conscious filters that connect to my five senses couldn't actually compute what they were seeing. They weren't really designed for alternate worlds. Perhaps this was why I perceived everything as three iridescent bubbles suspended in a baby-pink atmosphere.

But now I was going to find out from a reliable source exactly what had happened last night and what it was I'd seen. I followed the steps of my now well-practiced ritual meditation. It is difficult to meditate and settle into calm when you have a hundred questions flying around in your head and you're anxious to talk about it. I was going to have to let go of all of my swirling thoughts for the moment if I wanted to be able to connect in with my Guides.

Gradually, inward I went. My heart began to open, my mind became calm, and soon I was feeling very patient. Just being in this place felt so good. I began to allow the images from last night's vision to replay in my mind's eye. As I watched the review I spoke to them silently. *What was this? What happened?* Then I waited and waited...and waited some more. Hmmm, no answer? Okay, I was going to need a different approach.

I decided to go to a place within, where I often met with my teachers. I usually traveled a short walk down a path through a forest, which led to a small opening. There, I would sit on a single large flat rock and have conversations with whoever showed up. Different Guides would appear at different times. Today it was the female. She always had this incredible energy about her. She moved with fluidness, her long blonde hair easily reaching her waist and shimmering with golden hues. Her eyes were a piercing azure blue. Other than these few details, everything else was difficult to see. With these guys, it always seemed to be an either–or situation. Either they spoke directly within my mind and I saw nothing but blackness, or we would meet in my forest glade and I would see them, but all communication was nonverbal.

Her name, if I understood it correctly, was Adriana. I know it wasn't exactly that, but it was as close an interpretation as I could find. She didn't seem to mind the name. As soon as she was fully in front of me, I asked about the vision.

"What *was* that last night? What was I seeing? I need help with this because I don't understand, but I *want* to understand."

She kneeled down in response. As always, a look of love radiated from her kind and knowledgeable eyes. She held a closed hand out to me and slowly opened it. As her fingers spread out, I looked down, only to see absolutely nothing but her empty palm.

I fumbled around with the meaning of this for a moment. Usually—no, almost always—when they offered me a symbol, I would immediately understand its meaning. This, however, had me utterly stumped. I did know she was not asking me to take her hand. She wanted me to see her empty palm.

"Okay, I don't get it, Adriana. Please. Can you clarify what you mean?" Slowly she began to stand. "No! Wait! I need—" But it was too late. The vision was gone and now all I saw was the darkness behind my closed lids.

"Oh, for heaven's sake, you guys! What the hell does an empty palm mean? You know, if you didn't want to tell me, you could have just said no and that would have been the end of it. Geez, sometimes you guys can be real shits."

I know how I spoke to them seems harsh, but they truly felt like my brothers and sisters, and I always spoke openly and honestly about how I was feeling. From my point of view, even if I didn't say it, they would know what I was thinking anyway. I was just keeping it real.

Disappointment didn't even come close to how I was feeling about the whole incident. For the entire week, I attempted to gain some insight into what had occurred, but I kept hitting dead ends. They were not going to be coughing up any information on this at all. I had to simply chalk it up to one crazy experience and let it go.

I also began to be bothered by a subtle, nagging feeling that healing was not my calling. That's not to say I wasn't good at it or didn't enjoy it. Increasingly I knew, deep down in my heart, that healing wasn't my real purpose or path in life. It was just a stepping stone; the only problem was I didn't know what it was a stepping stone *to*. I still faced the biggest question that had plagued me all my life: What was my purpose in life? You would think, with all this intuitive information flying around, the Guides would at least answer some of the questions I had. I was beginning to realize that I had to discover some things for myself, like it or not.

When I began to share with my friends that I wasn't going to be doing any more healing for a while, they thought I had lost my mind completely. Any one of them would have gladly given everything they owned just to have the gift I was walking away from. This time even Brent, who was my biggest supporter and backed me in everything I wanted to do, thought I was making the wrong choice. But I knew I wasn't. This was another example of me knowing something deep in my heart and acting on it, while everyone around me thought I was crazy. It didn't bother me one bit, though; I had become quite accustomed to people's skepticism. What I did get out of this experience was a new motto, and every day I said it to myself: "You just have to follow your heart Cheryl...Follow Your Heart."

⚬ 5 ⚬

When All Else Fails, Give God the Finger

I still had a burning desire to be of service to the world. My heart wanted to give. Even though I wasn't sure of what my purpose was exactly, the rest of my life seemed to be falling in place. It had been nearly a year since my experience of the Light in hypnosis. I was more able to accept the strange gifts fate had handed me, and I was finally feeling at peace with it. It was pure pleasure to open my eyes each morning and actually look forward to the day ahead. I could only assume this was how normal, happy people lived.

Recently, I'd been finding it an absolute pleasure to have the house to myself each day. Every single kid-free day was a joy. I became pregnant at seventeen with my first son, Brandon. I had just turned eighteen a couple of months before I gave birth to him. In retrospect, that little baby boy saved my life. I put my old life behind me and dedicated myself to personal growth work in the hopes of offering my son a better life than I had known. My second son, Jaden, came along exactly ten years later. Their birthdays were only a week apart. I had spent my entire adult life raising little children; now, with both boys in school full time, I had finally regained a little piece of freedom. For a good portion of each day, I didn't have to be a wife or a mother. I could just be me, and I loved it.

It was now early afternoon and I still had a couple of hours before the boys would be back. I had completed everything on the checklist for the day, so I decided to lie down. Oh, the luxury of "single" life. I closed the curtains to darken the room and then happily slid under the sheets. As though I was making a snow angel, I waved my arms and legs as I lay on my back in the bed. Having the whole bed to myself made this even more of a delight. I was giggling like a little girl.

Even though I was genuinely tired, I was having a hard time getting the mental dialog to quiet down, so I decided to do some heart breathing. That is exactly what I needed to quiet the Chatty Cathy in my head, and finally I dozed peacefully off to sleep.

A short time later, my consciousness began to stir. My senses were suddenly abuzz, but I couldn't quite pull myself together. I had awakened, only to find that I was being hurtled through space. I was apparently traveling at a ridiculously high velocity. I was so confused that I wasn't even sure if I was awake. *What the hell? What is this?* I felt as if I were pinned to the bed by the sheer gravitational force of my speed. I knew I was on my bed, but at the same time I felt as though I was being hurled through space. I could only guess that this was the sensation an astronaut would feel as he was launched from the earth in a rocket—unable to move under the pressure of g-force. I saw nothing in my mind's eye but a void of blackness. My heart was racing wildly in my chest. I just had to double check. *Cheryl, are you awake? Ahhh...yes! You're thinking and you know you're not dreaming, so you must be awake! And for crying out loud, of course you're awake or you wouldn't be talking to yourself.* Hmmm, good point. So the fact was now established: I was indeed awake.

It was hard to think with the high-velocity pressure on the front on my body pushing me deeper and deeper into the bed. I was vibrating from head to toe. This wasn't just a pleasant tingling sensation either. It was a nonstop surge of high-voltage electrical current running through me as I was being forcefully shot through space. My eyes wouldn't budge and my arms wouldn't obey signals to move. I rationalized that this electrical current rushing through me must be interfering with my own neural electrical pulses. This must be why I couldn't move. *Maybe you're having a seizure?* I thought. *Oh for heaven's sake, girl, nobody has a seizure and thinks, "Oh, I'm having a seizure."* Okay, so it wasn't a seizure. *Well, maybe it's spiritual electroshock therapy?* I only had to think about that for a second. *Do you really think there is such a thing? Kind of masochistic, isn't it?* Maybe it was payback for telling them to F-off all the time—now that was a possibility. If I were a Spirit and I had the power to do this, I could think of a few people I might stop and visit with. *Okay, stop being funny, Cheryl. Really, this is not the time.*

My body had been hijacked by this electricity. I could do nothing else but talk to myself. I lay there for over fifteen minutes, unable to move. All I could do was experience it and wait for it to be over. Every muscle was taut as the surge flowed, and I had to make a concentrated effort just to breathe. Finally the intensity began to fade, and slowly but surely, breathing became easier too. Each muscle let go as the current faded away.

It was an enormous relief to have my body back. I felt amazingly relaxed, and before I knew it, I was sucked into one of the most vivid dreams I had experienced in a long time.

When I finally did awake, in full and for real this time, I sat up and looked at the clock. It had been only an hour and a half. I felt good despite the fact that I had just been shot through space from an astral slingshot and nearly electrified to death. I stared at the ceiling, focusing all my attention on my Guides. Did they really think they could get away with this? *You are so lucky you aren't here in the flesh, because if you were I'd kick your asses right now! You can't just come down and do whatever you want with me, you know. I do have rights.* I realized the ridiculousness of that thought. What were my rights? And even if I knew what they were, what was I going to do, call the karma police? I had to gather myself. *Just calm down, Cheryl. You know you signed up for this on some level long before you came here. You're really going to have to let go of being such a control freak.* Deep in my heart, I knew whatever it was that had just occurred was for my benefit.

That same night was the beginning of a two-week astral training boot camp. Each night it was the same kind of dream. Each dream had a slightly different scenario, but the main theme was the same: I was being taught how to fly. I could never determine who was instructing me. Most of the time I would be inside a room; only rarely was I ever outside. The sessions always started with me intensifying my energy field. Then I would slowly rise up until, nine times out of ten, my back would bounce along the ceiling. I felt just like a helium balloon. My arms and legs would spread out in a natural response to try to regain my balance. My invisible teachers would instruct me to use my core to control my motion, direction, and speed. They made it sound a lot easier than it actually was. The core they referred to was the central source of energy in my body, around my solar plexus. It ran along like a tube from just below my belly button up to the middle of my upper chest.

It took a few nights before I could get a good sense of my core. The way it worked was similar to a seesaw or teeter-totter. If you stand in the exact middle of a seesaw it will balance perfectly. If you tilt your weight, even to the slightest degree in one direction, it will begin to tip. The difference was that this teeter-totter also rotated in every direction. Instead of weight being the principle force of movement, the core used a concentrated energy force. It was rather like the feeling of squeezing your stomach muscles really tight. I had to squeeze the energy really tight to make flight happen.

Gradually, night after night, I was guided along as I learned to squeeze and balance the energy, and before I knew it I was pretty darned good at flying. They let me out of the room only a couple of times. The sheer force and speed at which I could travel was exhilarating. I loved these dreams and I was disappointed when the lessons drew to a close.

At the same time the training was taking place, I kept myself busy during the day with teachings of a different kind. I had become fascinated with the *energy thing* that had happened during my afternoon nap. I wanted to study it, understand it, and hopefully master it.

The very next day after the first energy thing, as I called it now, I was anxious to see if I could do it again. I tried to duplicate all the steps exactly as I had done the day before. I lay down in my bed, flat on my back. I positioned my arms alongside but not too tightly against my body. After inserting my little purple earplugs to prevent the sound of any tractors or horse trailers from disturbing me, I slowly began my heart breathing. It took me quite some time to drift into sleep; I had to breathe the anxious excitement out of me first. Sure enough, sometime later I awoke to the very same sensations in my body. I made sure I talked to myself enough to be able to thoroughly verify, without a doubt, that I was awake. And just like the first time, once the rush of energy had passed, I was immediately unconscious and thrust into a very vivid dream.

The only thing that was different from the first time was my attitude when I awoke. *Oh my God—it worked! I did it! Something has actually happened here!* Even though I didn't have a clue as to what it could possibly be, I was stoked!

I started my research online. It was difficult to find much because what I experienced was so vague and it didn't really fit the bill for anything concrete. The only thing that came even remotely close was an out-of-body experience, or OBE for short. From what I read on the Internet, there was a big surge of energy right before the astral body separates from the physical body. Also, a person could easily be sucked into a dream if they didn't get away from their body quickly enough once they were out. The way the energy surge was described didn't match the type of energy surge I experienced. I'd felt like I was already going somewhere when it came on. The information I found also made it seem as if the person would get very close to sleep, but would remain conscious in order to facilitate the OBE. Only the body was tricked into thinking it was asleep.

It didn't matter to me. This was close enough. I immediately went to the largest metaphysical bookstore in our area to get my hands on some good out-of-body guidebooks. I read with fervor. I wanted to get the basics down and get practicing so I could gain some control over the energy thing. I was positively ecstatic at the thought of being able to escape my body at will. I wanted to learn this as quickly as I could.

Getting out of my body wasn't the only thing on my mind, though. It had been months now since I had given up the healing work. I had been waiting for Spirit to tell me what I was really here to do. Every day I asked my Guides about my purpose, and every day went by without an answer. I saw many pictures and symbols when I did ask, but there was nothing solid to go on. I so desperately wanted to be of service, to be on a path of purpose, but the actual path itself evaded me. I was starting to feel frustrated and down about the whole effort. I was beginning to think that perhaps I was fooling myself by thinking I even had a purpose. The strange feeling inside me was a knowing and a doubting all at once, and frustration over these dueling feelings.

As I sat out on the porch one morning enjoying a steaming cup of coffee, I began to contemplate the entire *purpose* conundrum that I found myself in. At six o'clock in the morning, the world was still quiet. I always did my best thinking at this time of day. I was hoping I could make some sense of it all. I watched a pair of playful fillies out in the paddock. They were waiting restlessly at the shelter for the delivery of their morning hay and oats. I loved how the early-morning sun cast its long shadows, accentuating the definition of the horses' strong, muscular bodies. I knew the pair of them didn't wake up this morning wondering what their purpose was on this planet. And I wished for a time in my life when it could be the same for me.

I allowed my gaze to drift out to the distant sky. The longing in my heart turned into an ache, and my chest grew heavy with sadness. I started a one-way conversation with the Creator. He, She, It, They—whatever God was—needed to listen. I had to speak and I needed to be heard.

"Why can't you just give me a purpose in life? You've kept me around all these years—no matter how badly I wanted to come home, you wouldn't let me. It's so deep in my heart and I can't help how I feel. I need a reason to be. I *need* a purpose. I need to be of service. I'm beginning to think maybe you don't even have a purpose for me, do you? What more do I have to do? How much more do I need to beg and plead for you to tell me? Geez, what is the matter with you? And what's the matter with me? Am I not good enough to serve you? Tell me! Why won't you give me a purpose?" I paused, waiting as if an answer might actually come. As always, silence was the only reply, and it hurt. The fire in my heart burned. "Well, you know what? I've had it. That's right, *I've had it!* I'm done waiting. If you don't want to give me a purpose, then *screw you!* I'm going to give myself a purpose. I'm going to create my own path 'cause obviously you don't have one for me!" Then I popped my middle finger up to the air and gave God "the bird." "Screw you. I'll do it myself."

And as if in response to my cussing at God, one of the fillies let out a loud and boisterous whinny. It sounded a lot like laughter to me. In that moment, it felt as though the Universe was heckling me, but in retrospect, I can say it was the Universe bursting with joy.

There was no doubt that the time I had spent living on the streets and in the projects during my early teens had etched a streak of attitude into me. By eighth grade, I had been permanently expelled from school for fighting. We weren't even into the third term yet and I had been in more fights than I had fingers. They were done with me. I was a measly four feet, eleven inches tall and weighed all of ninety-five pounds at maximum, but I was tough. I knew there would never be a girl who could hit me as hard as my older brother did. And I was right. So I fought anyone and everyone I could. I was trying to pound the pain out of me. I was trying to beat the world back for beating me.

The best way to describe me then was angry, emotionally damaged, and very closed off. Everything about me emanated, "Fuck you and then fuck you some more." I could not allow one more thing to hurt me. I was purely in survival mode; if I wasn't fighting, then I was running. Of course, no matter how much or how far I ran away, I couldn't escape the feelings. The whole world saw me as the problem, and I saw the whole world as the problem. It was a Mexican standoff and I wasn't backing down. I wasn't going down without a fight.

I had my first cigarette when I was ten. I became instantly hooked. By the time I was fourteen, I had run away from home more times than I could count. I spent more of my teenage years living on the streets than at home with my family. The fighting, the drinking, and the drugs only worsened my sorrows and troubles. My poor mother had reached her wit's end. She just couldn't handle me anymore. No one could.

After a professional assessment, I was placed in the juvenile building of the local psychiatric hospital. I wasn't put there because they thought I suffered from a mental illness, but because they honestly didn't know what else to do with me. Since I hadn't been caught breaking the law, they could not legally put me in a juvenile detention center. It was the only other place that had locked doors, full security, and a team of educated professionals who were trained to handle difficult adolescents.

It was there where I earned the official, dubious title of "Detriment to Society." Psychologically, that stamp stayed with me for a very long time. During my stay, two other girls and I staged a midnight coup, beating one of the nighttime staff members and locking her in the time-out room. Certainly it was not one of my best moments in life.

If anyone, even just one person, had taken the time to look past my snarling teeth and vicious guardedness, they would have seen the wounded little girl I really was. My heart was bleeding on the inside and my spirit had been beaten nearly senseless. I was a *clairsentient* child living in a really messed-up world. My faith in mankind was lost. The only way to protect myself was to close my heart and keep everyone at bay. It was the only way to stop the flood of feelings and knowings and try to prevent any more pain.

But as with all good fairy tales, I did survive it. I ended up dedicating my life to spiritual and personal growth work. I could have stayed hurt and angry. I could have remained a "detriment to society." Somehow, though, my heart knew better. I only ever wanted to do good in this world, and the only way that was going to happen was if I created the opening for it. So I worked on healing both myself and my relationship with God. And as I've said before, to know our own darkness is to know our own Light. I figured I must have a whole lot of Light yet to shine!

⋘⊙⋙ 6 ⋘⊙⋙

Don't Answer the Voices Out Loud, Ever!

Clearly, I still had work to do on my relationship with God. It's not that I was outright angry; I was just a bit pissed with Him about the purpose thing. I had such a way of putting my foot in my mouth. I don't know how many times I had regrets and thought to myself later, *I wish I hadn't said that.* Well, this was one of those moments—I regretted the things I had said to God. Still, true to my nature, once I say I'm going to do something, I do it. I now had to show God I deserved a purpose and I could find one, with or without Him. It had been a week of heavy thinking and I still hadn't come up with anything solid. I'd had a couple of ideas, but my heart didn't feel it.

Yes, genius me had given the finger to the Creator of the entire universe and told him to go screw himself. *Brilliant, Cheryl, yeah... you're brilliant. Now what, big mouth? I think you're on your own with this one.* I went back to the Internet to look for ideas once again. Then it flashed through my mind like a lightning bolt. My heart did a wild patter and I could feel all the cells in my body respond. *Holy crap! That's it!* I started my search anew, but this time I knew what I was looking for. I began typing it into the search engine. I was going to look for a hypnotherapy school!

Why hadn't I thought of this earlier? It was so obvious. What better way to be of service to the world than to help people using hypnosis? I knew hypnotherapy worked because it had changed my entire life. Not that I expected everyone to have an angelic experience—far from it. But it had helped me get rid of some deep-seated beliefs I previously hadn't been able to shake.

I knew more about psychology than most people with degrees, and I had personally experienced a litany of trauma. With my intuition now fully functioning again and my passion for personal growth and healing, hypnotherapy was perfect.

I found all the schools in my area and even a few in the United States, since I was only five minutes from the border. I wrote all their names on a piece of paper and headed off to meditate. I held the paper in my hand as I sat cross-legged on the floor. Once I was in and connected, I began to repeat the name of the first school on my list. My intention was to connect with each school on an energetic level to see what they were like and if I resonated with them. One by one, I made my way down the list. The results of this procedure surprised even me—it worked like a charm! Only one school had given me an acute tingling sensation—the Coastal Academy of Hypnotic Arts & Science. It felt higher and lighter than the rest. I knew this was the one.

I went back to the computer and plugged in the name of the school. When I read over the website, I got the very same feeling. They had been teaching for years and had even taught international students. Perfect, I thought—big enough to be recognized for their teaching, yet small enough to be personal. The last step was to talk to them. Being the impulsive and impatient person I am, I called the school immediately.

The voice that answered had a smooth, calming tone, and I closed my eyes as we spoke. I needed to concentrate on the energy

I was feeling. I didn't want to be swayed by sounds or words. The energy was my only concern. I could feel the integrity and genuine passion for healing. This energy was motherly and very nurturing. I was speaking to the head director and facilitator, Leslie McIntosh. I liked this woman! That was enough for me. I enrolled right there and then for the next set of intensive full-time classes. I knew my choice was the right one and I was over the top with excitement.

A couple of weeks remained before class started, so I continued my studies of OBEs and the energy thing. To my dismay, none of what I was learning from the books or the Internet was actually getting me out of my body when the energy thing occurred. I tried to roll out of myself, to sit up and to push myself out—nothing worked. I tried to squeeze my energy just as I'd been taught in my dreams, but that had no effect either. I couldn't even get a leg raised. I was utterly perplexed. If this energy thing wasn't the beginning of an OBE, then what the heck was it?

I came up with a plan for an alternative approach. I was determined to figure this thing out. As usual, I lay down on my back. I always had to fidget and adjust myself a little before I felt perfectly comfortable. I had tried doing this while on my side a few times, but all I got out of that was a good nap. I had also added some things into the routine by now. I used my own variation of the techniques I had learned in the OBE books.

I would imagine or feel energy moving within my body. I would start at the center of the pads of my feet. Slowly, I allowed the energy to swirl and build. I had gotten pretty good at this because it felt as though it was really happening. From there I would let the energy flow up my legs and into my torso. First one leg, then the other. I took the time to feel the energy moving, inch by inch. Once it had made its way to my upper chest and through my heart, I would have it flow down my arms and into the palms of my hands. There the energy would remain, swirling. Of course, the energy also flowed up into my face and around my scalp, where it would finally settle at my crown. There it would swirl as well.

Once I had laid out the energy circuits in my body, I would begin the heart breathing. Just as I did when I meditated, I kept the thoughts at bay until I was fast asleep. As expected, I regained consciousness when the huge torrent of energy seized my body. I had become quite accustomed to it now and I fully relaxed into it. I allowed the energy to flow fully while I was forcefully propelled through space. Breathing was always easier when I relaxed.

Now it was time for my plan. Quietly and gently, in my mind, I called, *Dad? Dad, are you here?* I wasn't going to rush any part of it, and I waited patiently. *Dad, I would really love to see you. Are you here?* Over and over I called out to him, but there was no sign of his presence. As a matter of fact, there was never a sign of anything in here. I just flew through space as the electrical currents flowed. I felt a little sad and discouraged. It's not that I had expected him to be there, but I had really hoped he would show. However, that was not to be. The whole experience ended as it always ended: I was sucked out into a vivid dream.

In this dream, I found myself inside a different house on our farm. I was telling the boys and my husband to get back, get away from the window. I knew something was going to happen but I didn't know what. Everyone took cover and I ducked in behind an armchair. For some reason, I suddenly stood up. At the very same moment, a large explosion tore its way through our front window. My skin was savagely assaulted by hundreds of shards of glass as they shot into the room. I was filled with panic and fear, calling out to my husband and running over to show him my injuries. I obviously needed help. But when I held out my arms I was stunned. What should have been a hundred shards of broken glass in my skin was now an intricate array of gems and jeweled stones. It was dazzling and beautiful. The colors shimmered and sparkled as I rotated my hands and arms to look at them. Their beauty and the patterns they created on my skin were amazing. Then I awoke. It wouldn't be until much later that I would understand the significance of that dream.

I didn't give up on trying to call out to someone while I was in the energy thing. I tried several more times, calling my father, my Spirit Guides, the archangels, and anyone who might possibly come to visit. It was all to no avail. I was alone in the void. Completely and utterly alone. Now what?

I had to put aside my energy studies when my hypnotherapy course began. When the facilitator had said it was intensive, she wasn't joking. Each day was packed with learning and practice, and every night was consumed with studies. I had no time to think about the energy thing, but I always made time to meditate, even if I only had twenty minutes. I was not going to give up my connection with my Guides for anything. I felt like my brain might actually burst from the copious amount of information I was trying to stuff into it, and meditation was a reprieve. I'd always had a sharp mind and a knack for learning when I applied myself.

I thought back to another day, about a year earlier, when I was working at the computer in the kitchen of our old farmhouse. The house itself was small and the kitchen was the only room that afforded extra space. The walls, cupboards, and floor were all the same shade of blond wood. It was my second-favorite room in the house. Since the guys all hung out in the living room, it also offered me a bit of solitude.

I had found myself with nothing to do and was fishing around on the Internet for some intuition tests to try. Somehow I ended up on an IQ testing site. Temptation got the best of me. Even though I was a bit nervous to know what my IQ was, I was too curious not to take it.

For twenty minutes I plugged through the ridiculous questions on the quiz. A lot of it was mathematical mumbo-jumbo and I hated math. I had never even finished school, though later on I received a general education diploma. When I'd started thinking about going to university as an adult learner, I had to do testing to determine my level of education. The tests concluded I had university-level English and a sixth-grade-level math. That had made me laugh. Now I was taking an IQ test? If it came out any higher than seventy, I would be surprised.

Into the IQ test I dove. Diligently, I completed the questions to the end. I hit the submit button to reveal my score. My eyebrows popped up in response to what I read. Was this for real? I called Brent into the kitchen to take a look at my results.

"Hey hon, look at this. I just did an IQ test and look what it says." I smiled up at him proudly.

He leaned over my shoulder to take a look. I pushed myself over to the side, not just to give him room to read, but because I really wanted to see his reaction. Brent and I were both competitive people by nature. I was certain his reaction was going to be more entertaining than the test itself.

He quickly read the screen. His eyebrows immediately furled and his nose scrunched up. "What? *That* was your result? It can't be right."

Oh, was I insulted! That wasn't the reaction I had been expecting. "What do you mean, that can't be right? I took the damned test and this is what it says. It's right!" The way he acted, it appeared he thought I was mentally challenged. "If you think it's wrong, then take it yourself, smartass."

"Don't worry, I plan to. Here, move out of the way," he said, practically pulling the chair out from under me.

I happily relinquished my seat to the intellectual bully. So what if he was gifted at math? So what if he had completed high school? Jerk. That didn't give him any excuse to act so surprised over my results. I knew I was smart.

Methodically, he made his way through the test. With his pencil and paper in hand, he carefully calculated each question. I noticed he took longer on the questions that didn't pertain to math. Finally, he was finished. I had sat on one of the chairs behind him the whole time, watching over his shoulder. I didn't want to miss it when he received his results. With a final click of the mouse, his score was in.

"Ha!" I yelled, pointing at the screen as I jumped out of my chair in excitement. "Oh yes! Ha, ha, ha!" I couldn't help but gloat. He deserved it! "Think I'm stupid, do you? Well, if I'm stupid, then this makes you a complete nitwit!" I laughed so hard I had tears in my eyes. Mercy wasn't my strong suit.

Now he was furious! "How the hell is that even possible?" he demanded to know. He was truly shocked. I'm sure he believed his education would give him an edge over me, but it hadn't. Now he needed answers. "Come over here." He pulled my chair up beside him so we could both look at the screen.

"Cheryl. Would you stop laughing. Please." He made an effort to sound polite.

I tried to suck it up a bit as I wiped my watering eyes. I was grinning so hard it hurt my cheeks. A couple of little jerking snorts escaped me. He glanced over at me, sneering. "All right now?"

"Uh huh!" I grunted. I knew if I spoke I would break out again. I was still grinning hard.

Back to the beginning of the test he went. He scrolled through the first couple of questions until he reached what he thought was a good one. He looked back over his own papers, searching for the answer to the question. He held his mathematical scribblings to his chest as he handed me a fresh piece of paper and a pencil.

"Okay, now. What's the answer to this question?" He pointed down to the paper, suggesting I should begin working it out.

I looked at him and then the screen. I read the question, which of course was a math question. I quickly scanned down through the possible choices.

"D," I stated. Then I looked at him.

"What? What do you mean, 'D'?" He was mocking my voice sarcastically as he said the letter. "How do you *know* it's D?"

"Ah, I don't know. I just think it's D. It's the only one that looks right," I said innocently.

His lips pursed and he moved on to another question. "What about this one? What's the answer?" He was completely agitated now.

"A," I answered. "Am I right?"

"Cheryl, that doesn't count!" I guessed I was right because he started to throw a little fit now. "You can't just do an IQ test and give the answer without showing how you got the answer!"

"Why can't I?" I retorted. "It didn't ask me *how* I got the answer, Brent. It's asking what *is* the answer. And that's the friggin' answer!"

"But the point is you don't really know what the answer is. So, what? You're using your sixth sense to do an IQ test and you think it should count?"

I sighed. "This *is* my mode of operating. This is how my mind functions and how I get through the world and my life. Yes, my IQ is high, and I can't do the math to show why it's high. I get my information from a different source is all. That does *not* make it invalid. It's simply how my intelligence functions!"

"It doesn't count," he stubbornly insisted.

I got up and kissed him on his bald head, then whispered in his ear, "Don't be jealous, baby, that's just how I roll. It's not my fault God made me smart and you...not so smart!" Then I playfully poked my finger into his ribs and walked away, laughing.

Smart or not, I found the hypnotherapy course to be a challenge. I wanted to do my very best and learn everything as thoroughly as I could. I practiced as much as possible outside of class, hypnotizing anyone who was game. I felt very confident by the time I graduated. I had definitely made the right choice of schools, and I knew I had received every tool I needed to begin my own practice. I was now officially a Certified Clinical Hypnotherapist.

As with nearly any business nowadays, if you don't have a website, people aren't going to find you. I knew I had a great business sense, much of which came from the wide array of skills I had learned from previous jobs. I called around to a couple of graphic designers to get pricing on a small website. To my dismay, the quotes were far out of my budget. As usual, I was going to have to do it myself.

On to Google I went to begin my training on how to build a website. Within three days I had learned all the basics of HTML and CSS. In order to make my site look good, I also had to learn the basics of graphic design. I purchased a copy of Adobe Photoshop and started Googling tutorials to learn what I needed to do. In less than a week, I had a slick and professional-looking website. I also had a new passion. The graphic design and challenge of coding fed my appetite for creating and problem solving.

I quickly built a successful hypnotherapy practice. Within a short time, I had grown so busy that I needed to move my practice out of my home. I found a great little office in a local alternative health building and shared it with a fellow hypnotherapist, Kim Boudreau. I had met Kim when she taught a small course on energetic cording at Coastal Academy, and we hit it off right away. I couldn't think of anyone better to share space with.

It had barely been six months into my new career as a hypnotherapist and I loved it. I think the majority of my clients liked me too. I was so busy that most of my time at the office was booked. The burning desire to be of service was strong within me, and I wanted to help everyone I could. However, there will always be people whom you cannot help, and it never failed to bother me when I encountered one of them.

One night, I had an early-evening appointment and I was running a bit behind. As I pulled into the parking lot, I knew I would have just enough time to prepare the room and settle myself before my new client arrived. The only available parking spot faced the road. Directly across the road was a brand new metaphysical store. It had been open only for a few weeks. As much as I loved going into these types of stores, I had tried to stay away. I knew I would not be able to resist buying something. Even though my business was good, we were still just making it. I didn't have the extra cash to spend. I rolled into the parking space and turned the car engine off.

"Go in the store," spoke the voice, loud and clear.

I was surprised to hear one of my Guides. Before this, I had only ever heard them during meditation. I sat there looking across the darkened street to the well-lit store on the other side. Alluring chimes and crystals hung inside the window. Besides that, I couldn't for the life of me figure out why I should possibly go over there, especially when I was already late.

I replied out loud, as if whoever had spoken was sitting in the passenger's seat beside me. "What?" I questioned. "I only have a couple of minutes. I don't have time for that, you guys." I began to gather up my things.

"Go in the store," the voice repeated, in the same tone and manner as before. It wasn't pushy or demanding, just matter-of-fact.

"Ahhhh!" I groaned, feeling frustrated. "I can't! I have a client coming and I have to get ready!"

I had my bag on my shoulder now and the files in my hand. I was halfway out of the car when the voice spoke again. "Go, Cheryl."

"Okay, *fine*! I'll go for shit's sake, but if I'm late I'm blaming you!" I slammed the car door shut. At that moment I realized I had been talking out loud, to myself. *Oh boy.* I felt a rush of blood to my face. *I hope no one heard that!* I clicked the button on my keychain to lock the doors as I quickly scanned the poorly lit lot. There wasn't a soul around. *Oh, thank God, no one heard that!* Immediately afterward, I felt a chuckle that certainly was not my own. "Ha, ha. Funny," I said sarcastically aloud again as I headed across the street.

I made my way into the brightly lit shop and immediately heard a familiar voice. Soft billows of my favorite incense seduced my nose. I had always found the scent of Nag Champa intoxicating.

Books lined one entire wall. The urge to start scouring the shelves was strong and I had to refrain. I just didn't have time for that right now.

"Look, there she is! Speak of the little devil." Kim's usually boisterous voice filled the entire store. I looked past all the tempting knickknacks in the shop to see Kim standing at the till, talking with the store's owner.

I acknowledged my friend with a nod as I approached and smiled at the woman behind the counter.

"I was just talking about you!" Kim announced. "I was telling the lady here I know someone who is awesome at building websites."

"You were? Why?" I was taken off guard. I don't know what I had expected, but it certainly wasn't this. I was trying to keep my eye on the ladies I spoke with and not on the product.

Kim scooted a couple of steps back from the counter and pointed down at the back of the cash register. There hung a small handwritten sign reading, "Help Wanted – Looking for knowledgeable and experienced web designer. Please submit resumé at the counter."

I had to admit that I immediately felt a warm, bubbly feeling wash through my body in response to what I had read. Kim was on a talking spree now, telling the woman how great I was at building sites.

The shop owner, Patricia, asked me a few questions, and before I knew it, I agreed to do it. I don't know why I did. I was very busy with my family and a successful hypnotherapy practice, and I didn't have a whole lot of extra time. I explained I had a client waiting and I had to leave. Understanding my hurry, she passed me a business card and asked me to call her tomorrow. I looked down at the card and then everything stopped. A violet-colored swirling image unlike anything I had ever seen before grabbed and took hold of my mind. It was incredible. My head was literally ringing.

"What is this picture?" I didn't even look at her as I asked. My eyes were glued to the image. I was completely mesmerized by it.

"It's a fractal," Patricia proudly replied. "It was intuitively made for our store."

I had no idea in that moment that the next step in my destiny had just come for me.

⚜ 7 ⚜

*B*irth of Angels

Within a week, I had begun working on the store's website. I loved doing web design just as much as I loved doing hypnotherapy. When I was pregnant with Jaden, my second child, I had gone back to school and completed the twelfth grade. I was able to get only one term of college English in before the finances ran out. Doing marketing and public relations was my big dream at the time, and I was devastated that I couldn't continue. I'd say to myself, "Maybe someday, Cheryl," even though I was sure that day was never going to come.

Websites were a magical blend of creativity, artistry, coding, and problem solving, with just enough marketing and public relations thrown in to really get my juices going. I loved it! As with most things, I was completely self-taught. It was reminiscent of the movie, *The Matrix*, where characters would plug a cord into the back of their heads and download what they needed to learn. That was how my brain worked. It was as if anything I needed to know was instantly downloaded and at my disposal. If I needed to know how to do something, I would head off to the Internet for instructions. I'd only have to read it once and I got it. I used to joke with everyone that I received a graphics and web design degree from Google. But it really wasn't much of a joke.

I hadn't been working for long on the store's website when one day Patricia suggested I try making fractals myself. Neither of us knew it at the time, but Spirit was using her as an instrument to relay a very important message.

I hemmed and hawed about it for a couple of days. Fractal art is a form of computer-generated art, often called algorithmic art because of the calculations it represents. The images I was going to make were visual representations of fractal geometry, and when it came to anything mathematical, I was terrible. I highly doubted I could do it, but I had a hard time resisting the challenge.

I spent over a week trying to find the right program for me. It was a good thing many of them had free trial versions or I would have been out of funds the first day. I was trying to hunt down a fractal-generating software program that I resonated with. The mathematics nearly repelled me, but there was something else inside of me prodding me on. I had the feeling that if I could just find the right program, I could do this. And I was right.

Immediately I found that working the program was a snap, which really surprised me. I felt as though I already had the knowledge of how to work it before I even had it in my hands. My problem was that the fractals I produced were ugly! I knew I was very artistic and had a good eye, but I found the fractal art I was making almost repulsive. Was it because I wasn't very good at math?

To work the fractal program, I had to select a formula to apply to the base fractal called a Mandelbrot. Each time I added a formula, I would sit and wait as a new image rendered on the screen. I quite enjoyed the process. My perfectionist and control-freak tendencies were rendered useless; I had no control over anything. Whatever I got on the screen was what I got. I couldn't perfect it any more than that.

One morning during meditation I decided to ask why all the fractals I made were so terribly unappealing. I sat up on my bed where I could get my body into the warm stream of sunshine coming through the window. I loved how fresh my bedroom felt when it was bright and sunny outside. I was feeling good about everything in my life right now, and I went into my inner realm easily. I wanted to make my fractals prettier, but I just didn't know how. I was sure a little guidance on the subject could help.

By the time I finished my basic grounding and heart breathing, I was in pretty deep. I could always identify this depth because my body would feel altered in some way. Today I felt as though I had nothing but an expanded upper body and my extremities had all but disappeared. I knew I was still sitting cross-legged and my hands were lying gently on my thighs, but I couldn't feel them. I was deep within the vastness of my consciousness with only an upper torso and head.

I recalled a vision of myself sitting at the computer, working my fractal program. I envisioned one of my creations on the screen and allowed the feelings it invoked in me to flow. Then I inwardly asked for help.

"How do I make these fractals? I want to do them better." I quieted myself for the reply. Within seconds, the memory of Patricia's words flooded back to me. "It's a fractal," she had said. "It was intuitively made for our store."

I instantly understood what that meant and I felt excited about the answer. I was to use an intuitive process. Using my conscious, thinking mind was getting me nowhere. Then it occurred to me that I didn't have a clue how to do this intuitively. Someone must have heard me thinking, because the answer came even before I could ask for instructions.

Lance, the very first horse I had healed, came into my vision. My energy felt as if it smiled in response to seeing him. I loved that guy and I had a lot of gratitude for his part in my learning. The vision expanded a little more and I could see he was out in a paddock. Then the images faded and I was taken back to an awareness of myself sitting in my room.

I gave myself a moment to process it. I felt a rush of joy when I had the puzzle pieces put together. My Guides wanted me to use the same technique they had taught me to connect with Lance and all the other animals, which made perfect sense. I was to connect intuitively using words or names. I was excited now—I already knew how to do that!

The next thought in my mind questioned what or who I should intuitively connect with. Immediately, the answer followed. In my mind's eye I saw one of my invoices to the store for website work, at the top of which was the name of my company, Spirit's Way Designs. Now I was even more excited. I would not have thought of this on my own! I had to be careful not to get too agitated or I might pull myself out of meditation.

I was anxious to try this out. Slowly and quietly, in my mind I began to repeat my company name. It proved to be tougher than I expected. Usually I would connect quickly to an animal or even a person. I soon realized I was having a hard time connecting because I was the company and I was a major part of the energy. It was similar to a person who has never seen their own reflection. The first time they are given a mirror, they don't know they are looking at themselves. And that's how it was for me—I was trying to find and feel my own energy. I was just going to have to work a bit more at connecting with it and myself.

Once I felt the energetic hookup, I sat in it for a few minutes. I wanted to make sure I would keep this connection even after I pulled out of meditation. Then, mindfully, I allowed my body to stretch and I quietly walked out to the kitchen. I sat down at the computer and opened the fractal program. Just to get re-centered, I took a couple of heart breaths with my eyes closed.

As I began to work on the fractal, I had a very clear sense

of which formula to use. I applied it and waited for the image to render on screen. Over and over, layer after layer, the formulas were applied and the images rendered. Sometimes I would pause and say the company name silently in my mind to keep the connection strong. I found it hard to work this intensely for much longer than a couple of hours. I was tired, but I knew this fractal wasn't complete.

Every morning I worked on the fractal. I scheduled the hypnotherapy and graphic design work in the afternoons and evenings. After a few weeks, I began to wonder if the fractal would ever feel like it was finished, and I started to have doubts about whether I was doing the right thing. I was seriously beginning to question whether I should even be doing fractals at all.

It was coming up to the two-week mark, almost to the day. I had to make a concerted effort not to allow my feelings of doubt to interfere with what I was trying to accomplish. As usual, I connected into the energy of my company while I meditated and then came out to the computer to work. After several hours, I had already applied many formulas, and it was getting near time to call it a day. I had clicked the button for the last image, and I watched the screen as the image rendered out. I felt a slight lightness as I watched it slowly appear. It wasn't finished when a strange sensation ran through me. It was as though a gong had been struck inside my head and its vibrations had traveled down my spine—distinct and vivid. I hadn't expected this reaction and it caught me off guard.

Gradually, my eyes began to register what I was seeing on the monitor. Lines and shapes, repeating themselves into infinity. Warm yellow and brown tones resonated within me. Quickly, my mind took in the fullness of the image and an instant emotional reaction followed. I saw what looked like a large angel in symbolic form. In an endless stream, rising up from the cosmos beside the angel, were thousands of smaller angels. My chest tightened and tears began flowing down my cheeks. A rush of information from within the image flooded my mind. I was completely overwhelmed.

These weren't just any angels; these were my angels, and they wanted me to know they were with me. It was a reminder that I had never been and never would be alone. I was deeply loved and cared for, always and forever. They held me closest in those times when I did not know if I could make it one more day. They worked to uplift me and support me, so I would not end my time here on Earth too soon. These fractal angels also held another message, a different message. And it was this part of the message that broke me down into a full sobbing cry. They were telling me that just as they were here uplifting me, I was here to uplift others. They wanted me to know that this is what I was meant to do. These fractals were my work and the angels were here to fully support me in doing it. This work was God's message and I could serve humanity and the world through it.

All I could do was cry, tears of both joy and release. The last of the lingering beliefs that I had no reason to be here were being washed away. I had no choice but to let that go now. Rivers of elation and gratitude flowed in between. My head rested in my arms as they lay on the desk. My body jerked with sobbing breaths. Every once in a while I would lift my head to look at this incredible image of love on the screen.

I'm not sure how long I sat at my desk crying, but it was a very long time. When I finally did manage to pull myself together, my eyes were swollen and puffy and my skin was molten and red. My sleeves were utterly drenched and I had to go change my top. I dropped onto the bed, feeling completely exhausted. I needed to rest now. I needed time to process the messages I received and what all of this meant to me.

༄ *8* ༄

When Aliens Come to Visit

I struggled with the idea that making fractal images was a part of my purpose and path in life. I couldn't understand how exactly they fit in anywhere or served anyone. I could feel a distinct energy coming from each of the fractals and it felt easy to tap into them intuitively. So I knew there was more to these than met the eye. Each morning after meditation, I would head off to my computer. Most of the time, I would simply tap into my Guides and create random fractals. My Guides were always there during the process, providing me with a clear yes or no when choosing formulas.

As I began hoarding quite a large collection of fractals, I also researched them to understand their significance and meaning. Why would Spirit want me to make these when I could be doing any other art? As usual, my logical mind needed to understand. I was starting to annoy myself with all this doubting. I headed off again to my favorite resource, the Internet. I was surprised by the sheer volume of information I found once I began to look for it. Every article I read took me deeper and deeper down the rabbit hole.

Even though all the math both repelled and bored me, I had

to dive in. I had to understand exactly what a fractal was at least. I learned that fractal mathematics was a type of geometry that described nature. The word *fractal* meant "self-similar" or "self-repeating." Everything in the natural world was created from fractal geometry, including humans and all living creatures, right down to our DNA and cell reproduction. It occurred to me that fractals were organic, living art. It was also interesting to discover that the math was so complicated it couldn't be done by hand. Mathematicians had to wait for the invention of computers in order to do the calculations.

This was an intriguing start and it fueled me further. I found studies by a Russian scientist, Dr. Pjotr Garjajev, and his group after the Human Genome Project failed to show significant differences between the DNA of humans and chimpanzees. In these studies, they found that noncoding or "junk" nucleotides of DNA actually arranged themselves in fractal-like patterns called 1/f noise. It was a significant discovery, since human DNA is composed of nearly 95% of this so-called junk. The studies suggested that junk DNA followed the same structure as languages, and researchers had discovered a grammar or syntax within the patterns that could form strings of words.

This Russian group conducted experiments in which they were able to reprogram parts of junk DNA sequences using modulated laser light. They were able to modify this laser light and even radio waves to have meaning using the syntax or grammar rules of DNA language. In other words, as long as they used the correct resonant frequencies of DNA when modifying the waves, they were able to reprogram junk DNA in living organisms.

The Russians also found that the copy of DNA information used to make an organism was not contained solely within DNA molecules. This genomic information was being stored nonlocally. The DNA molecule simply acted as a storage device that could read and write the genomic information from the nonlocal source field. The DNA was using the 1/f noise fractal patterning to send and receive the information in a holographic way. Also, because of the fractal patterning, large volumes of information could be contained and transferred within a very small space. Using electromagnetic and acoustic fields, they found they could read into this genomic holographic field. It was quantum physics at its best, and that wasn't all.

I had come across the work of a highly controversial US scientist named Dan Winters who had been outcast by his peers. Now, I didn't know whether what any of his peers said was true, but I have always tried to keep an open mind. Winters claimed he and his team had found proof that human emotions could also reprogram DNA. They found that the sonic waves of the heart followed "golden means," which meant they were actually fractal spiral waves of energy. Their studies concluded that DNA was able to read the fractal waves emitted by the heart. This held great significance for me because my Guides had put so much emphasis on opening, functioning, and operating from the heart.

I also discovered anywhere from thirty to eighty percent of crop circles contained basic fractal shapes in any given year. And there seemed to be plenty of theories out there as to the purpose of these circles. Research conducted by Freddy Silva showed that the circles actually radiated energy waves after they were created. I did wonder what the correlation between the fractal symbols in the circles and the energy waves that came from them could mean. I wished someone would pick up that part of the research someday.

The most relevant article I found was about the studies conducted by the University of Oregon in the United States. They found that when people looked at certain fractal images, they showed a major and positive physiological response. People just plain felt better. Their bodies also physically responded to the images. I was completely fascinated. I had a possible theory that because the subconscious mind speaks the language of color, shape, and symbols, these fractals were able to bypass the restrictions of the conscious mind and communicate directly with the subconscious. This held a whole new realm of positive solutions to healing both the body and mind, not to mention the spiritual implications.

All of these findings fueled my passion for my work. I had decided shortly after I received the Birth of Angels fractal that I would stop doing the hypnotherapy and focus on the fractals. I did continue with the web design, however—I needed the extra cash.

The hardest part in all this for me was showing anyone my work. I had lots of marvelous images but no one was seeing them. It took all the courage I had to bring out my art. I don't know what I feared most—that it wouldn't be good enough or that I would have to listen to people's judgments and criticism. I finally mustered up the guts to share my work with Patricia. Encouraged by her positive response, I began showing her the newest fractal creations as they came.

One day she pulled me aside to talk. Basically, she hit me with a Zen stick, so to speak. And to be honest, I needed it.

"Cheryl," she said quietly. "You have all this incredible artwork Spirit is bringing through you. This is truly a gift. It's a gift from Spirit to the world. You have no right to hide this away from everyone. You *must* share this with others. This is what it's meant for. Now, I don't know what's holding you back, but you're going to have to suck it up and get this out there."

She was absolutely right. I didn't have the right to hide it away, and on a deep level I had been feeling that. I had so much fear about sharing this work that I couldn't get past myself to do what I knew I needed to do. Showing my artwork to people would mean putting myself "out there," in the spotlight and open to judgments and possibly even rejection. Just thinking about it was hard to take. But Patty's words were exactly the wake-up call I needed; her words of encouragement gave me the strength I needed. I knew I first had to listen to the hundred and one excuses my mind fed me as to why I shouldn't do it. I had to examine them carefully and then lovingly send those beliefs on their way. I had to take action no matter how I felt inside.

The response to the art was far from what my fears had imagined it would be. Instead, many people resonated with it and truly responded to it. I was astounded that so many people could feel the energy that emanated from the fractals, just as I did. Before long I was doing personal fractals for others. I called them Soul Portraits. Some of the symbols that appeared in the images amazed me and often brought the owner of the portrait to tears. Angels, butterflies, or dragonflies were examples of the themes, things that held great personal meaning to the person. However, I was still going through the same set of doubts I'd had when doing the healing work. I still had fears about sharing the intuitive information I received, and I still sometimes doubted my ability to do this work. Apparently, I was the only one suffering from doubt because there was now a long list of people waiting to have their soul portrait done by me.

For some reason, at this time, I began to question my Guides during my meditation. I wanted to know more about the Beings and Spirits that were working for the betterment of us humans. I would get little bits and pieces of information, but as it was with anything important I wanted to know, it wasn't enough to go on. It was, again, another frustrating situation of me having to discover the answers for myself. Fortunately, I didn't have long to wait.

I was at the computer working on fractals. It was early afternoon in late July and it was uncomfortably hot. Both the boys were off with their dad running farm errands and I was taking full advantage of my alone time; now that it was summer vacation, I had very little time to myself. Thankfully, Brent did his best to take the boys whenever he could so I could have a little space. It was nearly impossible for me to meditate or work on fractals with the boys at home.

As usual, I felt connected and clearly guided as I worked on this fractal. Everything seemed to be going along smoothly. I had just clicked the button to apply the formula and was now waiting for the image to render on my screen. Depending on the fractal, some of them could take up to two minutes or longer to completely render. This was one of those extremely slow-loading fractals and I had to wait.

Dreamily, I turned my attention to the view outside the large kitchen window and stared out at the dairy cattle farm next door. It was such a dump over there. I couldn't figure out for the life of me why they couldn't fix it up, even just a little. I wondered how the cows felt giving milk in a place like that. Shaking my head at the thought of it, I turned my focus back to the computer.

My mouth fell open slightly as the image began to register in my brain. My head pushed backward in an unconscious response to what I was seeing. *What the hell?* My hands started to shake and I jumped out of my chair, which sent it rolling across the wood floor. Even my legs were shaking as pure fear and shock pumped through me.

"No way...no *freaking* way!" I yelled. My natural defense mechanism to fight had kicked in. My self-preservation mode had been activated and I couldn't help it. Angrily, I jabbed my finger at the screen. "No, you *don't*! This was *not* part of the deal, you guys. *No*! I am not doing this."

Trembling and cursing, I stood at my desk as my finger swung through the air with every word. I was talking to both my Guides and the *thing* that had made an appearance in my fractal. "I'm not doing this. Did you hear me? You can all just *piss off*! I am *not* doing this," I repeated over and over.

With my hands on my forehead, I bolted outside to the covered porch. I had to think and get some air. I definitely had to get away from *it*. I'd been taken completely off guard. Never had I expected this—never! I started having flashbacks to my childhood...all those years of watching for UFOs in the sky...my father's training on how to discern between an alien craft and a regular human craft...every Sunday filled with aliens, their technology, their interactions with ancient civilizations, and, of course, abductions. Extraterrestrials were a common part of my everyday world then and I was scared to death of them. I was completely freaking out.

The fractal image continued to flash back into my vision as I struggled to understand. The computer had generated what looked like a side profile of a large, round-headed alien, with small lips, a small nose, and a large eye. The background behind it was black with little white specks that looked like stars. I couldn't get the image out of my head, yet I couldn't go back in the house to face it either.

What was I going to do? Sit outside until Brent and the kids came back? How stupid would that look? Me sitting outside, scared to go back in my own house because of a picture on my computer screen? I'm sure Brent would have gotten a good chuckle out of that, and my pride just couldn't handle it. We'd been bickering quite a bit lately and I didn't want to appear vulnerable or weak.

Not so tough now, are you? You're going to have to do something, Cheryl, you can't just sit out here. And besides, you're being ridiculous! It's just a picture, for Christ's sake. You really need to get your head together. You need to go ask about this.

I knew that much was true. I really needed to seek some higher council on this one. I contemplated just meditating on the stairs where I was so I didn't have to go back inside the house. But the small trickles of sweat rolling down my body reminded me it was much too hot to connect to anything out here. I had to go in.

Luckily, I had gone out to the patio on the side of the house, off of the dining room. I could make a beeline right to my bedroom and avoid the kitchen altogether. I sucked in a deep breath as I looked up into the air, at *them*, my so-called Guides. I squeezed my eyelids half shut and threw a dirty look at them as I shook my head. A few profanities rolled through my mind. I got up and executed my entry as planned. On the way to the bedroom, I stopped only to grab a small fan that was running uselessly in the empty living room.

My curtains were closed to keep the heat of the southern

exposure out of the room. They were thick and served their purpose well. I positioned the fan at my back, then settled myself on the floor. The breeze was light and refreshing, which helped to clear my thoughts.

It took a lot of heart breathing after the grounding before I felt like I could connect. My anger had relinquished its hold, and a deep sadness and disappointment had replaced it. If they really knew me as they should have known me, then they should have never put me in this position. So why did this happen? Why the alien? I didn't like feeling as though my trust had been betrayed. I'd expect this of any human, as that is our nature, but not of them. I had put all my faith in their hands and this—this ambush by an alien—is what I got in return?

I was concentrating only on my heart and breath. It was all I could do. I wasn't asking anything and, probably for the first time in my life, I wasn't mouthing off either. I followed my breath into my heart, and felt it expand and grow. Gradually, a gentle wave of understanding and explanation washed through me when I didn't expect it. Tears began to trickle down my face.

At last I understood the message that had just been relayed to me. They had given me a symbol of non-human beings that was nearly universal nowadays. The fractal was not denoting any extraterrestrial race in particular. That wasn't the meaning at all. I had simply misinterpreted it because of my conscious filter. I had filled in the unknown part of the meaning with what was already programmed in my mind from so long ago. I understood that I needed to bypass my beliefs and preconceptions about this symbol and intuitively tune into the image itself. This would allow me to properly discern what the energy of the fractal really was.

Essentially, this had been a lesson in trusting not only my eyes and what I saw, but also what I felt intuitively. It was a big lesson on many levels, not only about learning to use and trust my intuition to decipher things, but also not to jump into fear and survival mode so quickly. That part of my life was over now and I had to live in this new era. I had to draw from the now and not my past.

I took the time to let all of this information settle deeply within me, in every cell of my being. I shed a lot of tears in the process. I felt a great lightness in both my body and my heart, and sent my Guides all my gratitude and love.

Everything was fine for the first couple of days after the alien fractal episode, but then slowly my doubting mind took over. I again began to question my sanity and whether any part of this was even real. Although I had shown the fractal to a couple of people without incident or concern on their parts, I still wasn't okay with everything. I did not tell anyone why I had received that fractal—I couldn't even admit it to myself. After a few weeks had gone by, I had thoroughly convinced myself that it was all a figment of my overly active imagination. A crazy imagination I could live with, the involvement of extraterrestrials I could not.

It was now nearly three weeks later, and I was content with my new conclusions about my imagination. Thinking I had completely squashed any ideas of other life forms, I was happily working away on my fractals and soul portraits.

I usually went to bed as soon as the sun went down. Since it was summer, it was just a little past ten before I settled in for the evening. It was still really warm in the house. It had been sweltering hot that day, without so much as the smallest breeze in the air, and the night offered little reprieve from the heat. With only a thin sheet over me, I left one leg out to keep cool as I easily drifted off to sleep.

Sometime in the middle of the night, I awoke. Other than opening my eyes, no other part of my body moved. Strangely, right at the time I had been drawn out of my dreamy sleep, Brent had awoken too. Without saying a word, he slipped out from under the sheet and headed off to the bathroom. I tilted my head slightly to look out the window beside our bed. The curtains were open.

The window was large and took up the entire length of the wall. The bed was positioned parallel to it.

As I gazed out the window, I saw a brightness in the sky, indicating the sun must be starting to rise already. Yet I felt so tired still; it didn't feel like I had slept that long. From where I was lying, I was looking out the south window on an angle into the west. There, the sun was beaming through a long row of tall poplar trees that ran along the fence line of the yard, separating it from the large paddock on the other side. I was looking through the trees to the paddock and the sun, there in the west.

Slowly, the absurdity of looking at the rising sun hit me. I was looking out into the west, not the east where the sun rises. My thoughts began to swirl and I began to holler silently to myself. *Wake up, Cheryl, wake up!* I watched the glow as it moved from the ground straight up until it was half above the treetops.

My body was completely paralyzed. I didn't know if it was the fear that had done it, but I wished to God my body would move so I could run away. All I could do was stare at the orange glowing ball of light hovering beside my house—in the west! Insurmountable fear claimed every part of me as my heart pounded wildly in my chest. I began screaming for Brent with all my might, but my voice was only in my mind. My lips wouldn't work, my mouth wouldn't open, and I couldn't get the air to activate my voice. *Brent! Please come back, please! Help me! Where are you? I need you...please come back!* But he wasn't coming.

My eyes remained glued to the vision outside my window. This enormous glowing orange circle was surrounded by swirls of pure white smoke. Strange—if the light was orange, why didn't the smoke take on its color, too? Instead, the smoke was being lit up as if from a white light that emanated from the orange glow. I could not make sense of it and I didn't try to.

I knew exactly what it was. I had feared this all of my life and now here it was, outside my window. Did these aliens really think they were just going to come and take me? Not unless they killed me first! I began to yell at them in my mind. *I know you can damn well hear me. You have no right, absolutely* no right *to come in here. Don't you even think of it. Don't you* dare *come in here! Don't you* dare *touch me! I swear to God I will find you and kill you myself! You have* no right!

Two things happened at once. I heard Brent's footsteps returning. The moment he took his first step back into our room, the light vanished from the sky, and the room was thrown into darkness once again. Suddenly, I was released from my paralyzed state. I bolted straight up and ran across the bedroom to Brent, collapsing in his arms.

He had no idea what had just happened. He had gone to pee and returned to the room only to be jumped by a screaming, hysterical wife. I was moaning and crying and talking so fast that he couldn't make sense of anything I was saying.

"Whoa, whoa...calm down. Cheryl, calm down," he said as he held on to me.

"Brent...oh my God! They were here! They came here! They were right outside the window." I was still filled with panic and half crying. My body was shaking uncontrollably.

"Okay, all right. Now, who was here?" He continued to hold me, rocking, hoping to soothe me.

"*They* were here, Brent. Them." I pointed up to the ceiling. There was just enough moonlight that we could see our silhouettes in the darkness.

"Who?"

Oh God, he was going to make me say it, I didn't want to, but I had no choice. "Aliens, Brent. Extraterrestrials!" I pulled myself from Brent's hold and headed over to the window, where I pointed outside. "They were right there, over the trees in the paddock."

He sat down on the bed and stared out the window.

"The light was orange and had white swirling smoke. At first

I thought it was the sun, but it wasn't. And I tried to yell for you and I couldn't, so I yelled at them in my head. Why did you take so long? What were you doing in the bathroom all this time?" I was still talking rapidly.

"What do you mean, why did I take so long? I just peed and came back!"

I walked to the bed and sat down beside him to explain. "Hon, you were gone for over ten minutes."

"Uh, no I wasn't. It was only a minute or two."

Clearly, we both had a completely different perception of just how much time had actually passed. My mind was nearly overloaded now, and I hung my head down into my hands. I began to cry quietly. Instinctively, Brent began to rub my back to comfort me.

"There's nothing out there now, honey."

After a few moments I began to speak. "I don't know, babe. It was all so strange. The lights and the smoke. I mean, what was it really?" My logical mind had kicked in once again and my defense of doubt had returned. "I was half asleep when it started to happen. You know? Maybe I just got carried away with it. Maybe my imagination was overreacting. I mean, come on...really. It couldn't have been that."

I was fully talking myself out of it now. His hand rubbing my back felt so nice, and all I wanted to do was go back to sleep and pretend this had never happened. "I don't know what I was thinking, Brent. There's just no way...really...there's no way it was actually aliens!"

Suddenly a thunderous *bang* filled the air. We jumped off the bed simultaneously. The flash and sound of the explosion sent fear pulsing through both of us. The very second the word *aliens* was released from my mouth, one of the power poles, straight down from where I had seen the glowing light, had exploded on the street.

"Holy shit!" Brent said, awestruck. The house, drained of its power supply, left us in an eerie silence.

"I'm sorry!" I hollered. "I'm sorry, okay? It was aliens, all right? I admit it—I believe it now, okay?"

Brent chuckled nervously and then put his arm around me. "Cher? I think it's time you just started to believe."

I knew he was right.

The next morning Brent spotted a repair crew out on the road assessing the pole that had exploded the night before. He decided to take a walk down there to have a talk with the men to see what he could discover.

When he returned he was smiling. Obviously there was something humorous in all this.

"What's up?" I said.

"Well, the guys said a branch hit the power box on the pole and caused it to explode. The funny thing is, they can't figure out where the branch came from. There was no wind last night at all, and there isn't a tree within one hundred feet of that pole. They can't figure out how a branch could have blown that kind of distance without a massive storm." Now he was laughing. "That's a message for you, Cheryl."

I hung my head for a minute. I had to admit he was right. This had to be the end of the doubting. The end of denying things. I was going to have to start taking this stuff at face value. I was going to have to do something, because I had obviously become a magnet for the paranormal. Oh, if Dad could only have been here for this. Deep in my heart, though, I was certain he had been.

Brent and I discussed this major event off and on for the rest of the day. And I had to agree with the conclusion he had drawn. He pointed out that had they been "little gray aliens who abducted people," they would have simply abducted me. Whoever they were, they had no intentions of that; they had respected my wishes and had not crossed any physical boundaries. Brent thought they were just trying to get a message to me about my denial about them and my work. Everything he said resonated with me.

I went into the bedroom for a little private time. I had something important I needed to say. I sat meditation style, with my eyes closed, and I began to speak from my heart. I shared all my feelings with them. In my mind, I talked and talked and talked. I had pretty much gotten it all out of my system except for one thing, which was the most important thing.

I put my hands together in prayer. My eyes, wet with tears, were still closed as I began to speak out loud.

"Okay guys...I want you to know I accept this work, and I promise to do it to the best of my abilities in whatever way you ask. But you need to promise me one thing, and I mean it. You have to promise me you will protect me, you will *always* take care of me, and nothing ever can or will happen to me. I need you to promise, okay?" In response, I felt a warm tingle of energy run through me. I knew that was a yes.

Little did I know at that time that they were going to more than fulfill their end of the promise; nor did I realize just how badly I would falter in mine.

◦◦ 9 ◦◦

Ain't Nobody Telling Me What to Do

Things were starting to take off with the fractals. The word was spreading. I so loved being my own boss and working at something that held deep meaning for me. Building websites to keep the cash flow coming in was still very much needed. Having that bit of money was helping to take some of the pressure off the relationship, too. Not that money was the real cause of the problems that Brent and I had been having, but it was something he focused on so he didn't have to look at the real issues.

While I had been growing, changing, and embracing my spiritual path in a whole new way, Brent had been growing increasingly distant. Despite his support, love, and helpfulness, I could sense that he had been shutting down for several years now. Our relationship was in rough shape. The racehorse industry was cold, cruel, and saturated with people who were ruthless, not caring about anything but their pocketbooks. Each racetrack was its own community, its own little world. It was filled with fighting, backstabbing, double crossing, substance abuse, and unfortunately for some horses, physical abuse.

Brent was there because it was the only work he had ever known. His father had trained horses, and as soon as he was old enough to pick up a pitchfork to clean a stall, his destiny in the industry was set. He had made an attempt to get out of it and had left it behind him when I met him in the spiritual community, but eventually he went back to horseracing so he could provide for his new family. There wasn't big money in standardbreds as there was in thoroughbreds, but it was enough to feed and clothe us.

I grew to loathe his work and everything about it, especially the track itself. I don't know how many times I had come home crying my eyes out over what I saw there. Indeed, *loathed* might be too nice of a word. I had tried to encourage him many times, in many different ways, to do something else, anything else. I told him I didn't care if he worked at the corner store as a cashier, for crying out loud. Anything would be better than racehorses. But he couldn't leave. His fear of not having enough to live on and not having skills to do anything else kept him chained to an industry he didn't want to be in. The only way for him to survive it was to shut down.

He had become stoic and unresponsive, emotionally and spiritually severed from the world. Disconnected from his own self, he was also disconnected from me, and I had begun to have a hard time with it. To say I was unhappy in my relationship and home life was becoming a serious understatement.

Feeling there wasn't a whole lot left for me in my relationship anymore, I poured all my passion and energy into my work. I had a long lineup of soul portraits to do and just as much web work too. This partially helped to fill the hole my empty relationship had left me with. The children had no idea anything was wrong. Brent and I did our best to keep our quarrels private and maintain peace in our household.

One day, Patty invited me to give a talk at her store. I had suspected this was going to come; I just didn't know how soon. The thought of standing in front of a bunch of people to talk about something as scientific and mathematical as fractals scared the heck out of me. Well, that's what I told her anyway. I knew full well that it had nothing to do with the topic and had everything to do with the speaker. I was just plain scared out of my mind! I had spoken to a crowd of over five hundred women when I was doing multilevel marketing a few years before. That hadn't been a problem, because I wasn't talking about myself and my life's work. The thought of exposing myself in such a personal way terrified me. I did the only thing I could: I politely turned her down. Patty didn't stop asking, however, and eventually the asking turned into insisting. There is only so much nagging a person can take, and finally I succumbed to the pressure and agreed.

Two days before the talk, I stopped into the store to discuss her website, and Patty came up with a statement that set my head on fire.

"Now, Cheryl, when you come to do the talk, please wear something nice. You need dress pants or a nice skirt. It doesn't matter what you choose, but you aren't allowed to wear jeans."

I sat behind the counter just staring at her. "Not allowed?" I repeated to be sure I understood it correctly. Heat started building in the sides of my jaw, and it rushed over my cheeks in a fury. Thank God I had thick olive skin that didn't color easily or I would have been fire-truck red. *Did she really just say, "Not allowed"? Are you freaking kidding me?*

Now, I like to try to get along with everyone and do my best to smooth things over whenever possible. However, when it came to anyone telling me what to do or trying to be an authority over me, my natural inclination to fight it kicked in. No one tells me what to do. Ask or suggest that I wear something nice? Okay, I'll consider it. Offer to help me pick out something? Okay. I'm not a fashion diva, so some help would be great. But do not *tell* me to wear something nice and say that I am not allowed to wear what I want.

In her words, I also heard some of my old tapes from the past playing. *You aren't good enough. No one is going to like you as you are. You look and dress like a poverty case. If you want to be accepted, you have to change. You'll never be anything more than street trash.*

I couldn't help myself—I was furious. I was aware that my ego had been triggered and I was going to have to look at it, but I'd look at it later. Right now all I wanted to do was react.

"When have you *ever* seen me in pants or a skirt? It's not a black-tie event here, Patty. It's a casual evening talk in the store. I am who I am, and I wear jeans. Either people want to listen to me or they don't, and I highly doubt the fabric or style of my clothes is going to have anything to do with that!" I delivered my message in strong tones so she could not fail to see that I was extremely insulted.

Patty just stared at me, her expression unchanged and her hands folded together in her lap. Then she started in with a slightly condescending tone I despised. She came from a much different background than mine. I also think the fact that she had just converted from a Christian lady of the Church to a New Age spiritualist just a year earlier had a lot to do with her ways of thinking.

"You want people to take you seriously. It's vital you begin to create your image now because it's really hard to go back and change it later. And really, you can't be taken seriously in blue jeans. Presentation is everything." Her statement was so matter-of-fact.

I immediately rebutted. "People will be able to discern who I am and what I'm about. I am not standing up there as a phony. I have something from Spirit I want to share with people. That's all it's about. I've gotta go," I said, hopping off my chair and quickly gathering my things. I wanted to get out of there before I said anything I might seriously regret.

"See you Thursday, seven sharp," Patty called to me as I opened the door to leave. She was completely unfazed by my reaction.

"Yeah," I replied as I kept walking.

I didn't know what to do. People were already booked for the talk, so canceling wasn't an option. I had too much integrity to bail out at the last minute because of something so personal and petty. For the next two days I had to do a lot of inner work over that one small conversation. I knew I was projecting my stuff about authority onto Patty, and I had to deal with it by changing me, not her. So I tried to perceive this as a gift that provided me the opportunity to see my erroneous beliefs about authority and control, along with my fear of rejection and being seen.

By the day of the talk I had most of my issues worked out in my head. They weren't healed or gone, but I had at least addressed them. I knew I was going to have to work on them a good deal more before they would loosen their hold on me. I had also written a list of keynotes to refer to in case my nerves got the best of me and I forgot everything. Feeling somewhat prepared and more relaxed, I decided to lie down to catch an afternoon nap. I wanted to feel fresh and energized for my big event. Even though we were only expecting twelve people, it was still big to me.

With the curtains drawn, the darkness quickly invited sleep. I scarcely had time to think before I drifted off into a deep, peaceful rest. I wasn't sure how long I had slept when I was once again awakened by that familiar buzzing. My body just lay there, somewhat tense, as the energy flowed. *This is strange!* I thought. *I didn't meditate or do any heart breathing...how could this be happening?* I was perplexed because I had always believed it was what I did before I napped that caused this energy thing to happen. Today I had done nothing and it was running at full intensity.

I didn't know what do to because I hadn't planned anything and I hadn't intended for this to happen. I just wanted to get some sleep. *Now what?* I began thinking about how very little I knew about any of the things that were happening to me. Then came the next thought. *I hate being so stupid about everything!* Instantly, there was an immediate reaction of the energy flow within me. It had faded to a dull roar. *What just happened?* I put two and two together and decided to try something else. *Love.* I said it slowly in my mind. Sure enough, the energy kicked up a little.

I was surprised, but mostly ecstatic. This was the first time I had been able to do anything while in the energy. Absolutely everything else had been unsuccessful up to this point. Eager to discover a way to control it, I said the word *love* over and over until the energy hit its peak and could not vibrate any harder or faster. I took my time so I could really experiment properly. Then I let out a stream of negative words: *hate, fuck you, disgusting*, and so on. Sure enough, the energy slowed down to a light hum. I found I had to have a nasty intent behind the word in order for it to have a downer effect. If I could have smiled I would have been beaming. Although my body couldn't express it for me, I was filled with joy inside.

Next, I dropped all words and instead went with the two emotions, love and hate. The energy reacted in exactly the same way. Over and over, up and down, the energy fluctuated until my consciousness switched off and I was tossed into a dream.

Probably the biggest part of the mystery of the energy to me was how I could be conscious and then suddenly become unconscious, each time it happened. It was almost as if someone had a remote control and I was the device. When they clicked a button, I'd power on and gain consciousness. Then, as soon as they hit the power button again, I was out cold. It was indeed a strange experience.

The energy experience of the afternoon had left me with a much-needed high, which came in handy for my speaking engagement that night. I began feeling the jitters many hours beforehand. People say they get butterflies in their stomach before having to speak publicly, but I had a colony of wild bats trying to escape from mine. I was much more than a little nervous—I was terrified.

I arrived at the store as scheduled, wearing a lovely pair of jeans with a set of heeled boots and a classy blouse. To me, I was dressed nicely. Now, one would think I had worn the jeans solely for the purpose of rebellion, but I hadn't. I did want to send Patty the message she couldn't tell people what to do in that way. But I also wanted her to see that her beliefs and judgments of people based on how they dressed were not necessarily shared by others. The final reason for the jeans was a simple one: I felt deeply that I had to represent myself as I am. I felt I needed to connect with people as myself, as a real person, and I had to be as honest as possible. Putting on airs or a false façade would only create a separation. I just had to offer my heart and it would all be fine.

I was right. It went extremely well. The beginning was shaky, literally. I had some strange fluctuations in my voice and the paper trembled in my hand. Once I got going, though, my nerves settled and my words flowed. However, that successful first talk did not in any way diminish my fear of talking to groups. The fear of the spotlight was embedded deeply, and it was going to take a whole lot more than that to send it on its way.

During my meditation the next morning, I felt it necessary to give gratitude and thanks to my Guides, angels, and whoever else was giving me a hand while I was here on Earth. I was elated that I'd been able to step beyond my boundary of fear to do what I needed to do. I was proud of myself. While I was reveling in my self-praise and gratitude, an image entered into my inner vision of a deck of tarot cards with my fractals on them. *What is this?* I silently questioned. As I looked deeper into the vision, I understood they weren't actually tarot cards—they were oracle cards.

When I was about ten or eleven, I had taken an interest in my father's Rider tarot deck. I played with the cards all the time, reading the guide book and trying to do readings. When he saw that it was more than just a passing fancy and I was genuinely interested in learning how to read them, he decided to teach me what he knew. He explained the meaning behind the four suits, how the major arcana cards held more important messages, and he offered some tips on how to learn their meanings. He also pointed out details, such as if one of the characters in the spread was looking in the direction of another card, it gave the other card more importance. I not only cherished my lessons in fortune telling, but also that precious time with my father.

It surprised me now to see a deck of cards in my mind's eye, especially since my fractals were on them. Then a strong feeling washed over me, and the message was clear: Make a deck of oracle cards.

Instantly, I felt myself reacting. All the reasons why I couldn't flooded into my head. *Oh, you guys! Are you serious? There's no way I can make those! I don't have a clue how to do that. I can't do it!* Then I purposely pulled out of the vision. I didn't want to look at it anymore. I don't know what I was thinking. I suppose I believed that if I stopped looking at the image of the cards in my head, the idea would go away and that would be the end of it. It wasn't the end at all, though—it was only the beginning.

Over the next few months, Patty began having small psychic fairs on the weekends. I loved getting readings, so I didn't decline when she asked me to stop by. I was gradually starting to get used to the idea of leaving the house and being social. You'd never know it if you talked to me, but for years I had been an almost complete recluse. I only left the house when necessary, to get groceries, run errands, or keep appointments. Other than that, I always stayed within the quiet, private confines of my home.

When I arrived at the fair, people were entering the building in a steady flow. I sat down at the table next to Patty to take a peek at the list of readers.

"Who is the best reader here?" I asked. She always had the readers do a reading for her personally before she'd allow them to work at her store, so I knew she had a pretty good idea of who I should see.

"Go see her." Her finger slid down the list to point out a name.

"Jeannie Martin? Is she good, though, like honestly good?"

"Oh yes, she's a third-generation medium. You'll like her." She put my name down for the next appointment.

Fifteen minutes later it was my turn. I headed to the far end of the room, to the small table where Jeannie sat. On top of the purple cloth that covered the table sat a deck of tarot cards, a couple of unusual crystals, and a little tea light.

"Hello honey. Are you my next appointment?" She smiled up at me.

I looked down into a set of crystal blue eyes that radiated love. I liked her already. I nodded in reply and she motioned for me to sit down. She offered a quick rundown about how she did her readings, then started into a short prayer.

As she whispered her prayer, most of which I couldn't hear, I noticed a strong sensation in the palms of my hands. I clasped them together as if to hold the tingling inside. I didn't know what this woman was saying or doing, but she could move energy in a way I had never experienced before. Whatever it was, it gave me a great deal of confidence in the reading I was about to receive.

She began by talking about my grandmother, who was always around me. Readers, if they were the real deal, would always pick up on her. Then, surprisingly, she picked up on my dad. That earned her some extra kudos in my eyes, since most readers never saw him. She was not even halfway into the reading yet when she hit on the stuff I wanted to know about.

"You have some important work to do, sweetie." She was only half looking at the cards she'd laid out on the table. I was guessing they were more for show than anything else, because most of her reading was coming from her direct connection. The majority of the time she sat with her palms up and her eyes closed. She only opened her eyes to speak. "They're showing me you have lots of work to do here. Your work is very public somehow, isn't it?"

"Maybe it could be," I answered, "but it isn't yet."

"Oh, it's going to be. Now, I don't know what it is you do, but I'm seeing tarot cards here."

That shocked me. I sat there wide-eyed as she continued her reading. I knew she had been connecting with my guys, and now she had one hundred percent of my attention and respect.

"Don't buy into your fears, okay honey? That's important. Whatever your work is, it's going everywhere."

You would think that would have been enough to convince me to make the deck of cards, but it wasn't. It was excruciating to think about putting my work out there like that, on such a large and public scale. So many fears and doubts flooded my mind that I felt paralyzed. I desperately wanted to remain small and hidden. I didn't want to claim anything, especially my power. If I claimed my power, then I would also be responsible for using it. Stepping into that kind of role was much too far beyond my comfort zone for me to accept.

Spirit, however, didn't seem to care about comfort zones, nor did Spirit care whether I felt ready to fully claim my path and my gifts. My Guides were intent on making sure I would get the message about what I needed to do, one way or another. At first it was pretty benign and even humorous. I would run into people and they would ask, "Have you ever thought about doing a deck of cards?" I would smile and tell them yes, I was thinking about it. Maybe one person, about every week or so, would ask me. Then it became two people, then the number expanded to four, until nearly every day I was asked the exact same question.

Now, it wasn't so funny. I was failing to see the amusement in the situation. This was outright harassment as far as I was concerned. If Spirit were a person, I could have had them arrested for stalking me. I told them off all the time, but it never stopped them. I didn't want to do it. My answer was no. Why wouldn't they just accept that? God, I wished there were such a thing as karma police. I certainly would have called them.

By this time, I was in a quandary. Jeannie and I had become

good friends, so I asked her out for coffee, hoping to get some advice. We met at a small coffee shop just up the road from the store. At the back of the shop, where it was quiet and empty, we sat on a comfy sofa and armchair. I also liked the low lighting—it felt more comforting somehow.

"Jeannie, I don't know what to do," I told her, my coffee cup clasped in my hands. I was looking down at the small table between us, hoping that would keep my tears at bay.

"What's wrong, sweetie?" She was just so kind and motherly. If there were such a thing as angels in the flesh, she was surely one of them.

"I'm...I'm not doing what I know I should be doing." I looked up into her shining eyes. "I know I'm supposed to make a deck of cards. It's clear this is what they want, but I can't do it. I can't! And they won't stop asking me. They're driving me nuts and I don't know what to do." As hard as I tried to hold them back, a couple of tears fell from my eyes.

"Why can't you? This is your path, honey, your destiny. You were made to do this, and no matter what, the Universe will support you in doing it. So what's holding you back?" She reached over and took hold of my hand.

"I'm scared to death, Jeannie! I'm so scared I'll fail. I don't want to fail. I hate failing. And if I did fail, I wouldn't just be letting myself down, I would also be letting God down! I couldn't live with that! And I don't want to put myself *out there*. I'd be right out there for everyone to see. I hate being in the spotlight. I can't take it. I'd rather hide than be rejected. Worse yet, what if I succeeded? Then what? How do I handle that? I've been nothing my entire life. I don't know how to be anything else. And I also can't afford it. I'd need *thousands* of dollars to print cards and I don't have a penny to my name. We just make it, paycheck to paycheck, and—"

I probably could have gone on for another hour listing my fears and beliefs, giving her hundreds of reasons why I couldn't do it.

Maybe I was trying to convince her as I had convinced myself so she would agree with me. But Jeannie wasn't buying it. She'd heard enough and cut me off mid-sentence.

"All right, now, you listen to me," she said in a firm, motherly tone. "I know how you see yourself, but that's not what I see when I look at you. I see a beautiful, strong young woman with a beautiful, strong heart. I believe in you, honey. I believe in God. The Universe always picks the right person to do the job. For this job, they have chosen you! *You!* You have to accept that, and you have to accept yourself while you're at it. So you need to work on that, you hear? Now, as far as the money goes, I'll do whatever I can to help you. I can sell one of my campers or get a loan. I'll do whatever it takes to make sure you have the money you need. I believe in you."

My eyes grew wide and a swoop of emotions flowed. I had difficulty believing what I had just heard. She would actually go that far to help me! Of all the people in the world Jeannie could help, she believed in this so strongly she was willing to stake her personal finances on me. All I could do was cry. I was filled with a huge mix of emotions.

I cried off and on as I drove myself home. I was overwhelmed with gratitude for the support I had been given, not only from Spirit, but from my Earth angel as well. Oh, me of little faith. How could I have doubted them? And why would I let my fears rule me like that? I made a firm commitment to myself that I would never again let my fears hold me back. I saw clearly, no matter how convincing they seemed, that fears were nothing more than bullshit. I wasn't going to buy into my own mind games like that again. I renewed my commitment to walk my path in whatever way was asked of me. Heart in hand, faith as my guide, I would walk my path with as much integrity as I could.

10

The Fractals Get Personal

As luck would have it, if it can be called that, Jeannie didn't have to sell anything or take out a loan. Spirit provided the way; I suppose they just wanted to hear the *yes* word out of my mouth first. Less than a week after I had spoken to Jeannie, I ran into Kim, my former office partner. We talked a little about hypnotherapy first, but the conversation quickly changed into a discussion about the previous week. I was eager to tell her about Jeannie's offer of help and how I was actually going to do a deck of cards now. I explained every detail. I was still quite emotional about everything and my eyes watered as I shared the story.

"Huh," Kim said after I'd finished the tale. "Well, that was pretty nice of her, wasn't it?"

"Yeah, can you believe it?" I looked at her with amazement.

"But you know what, Cheryl? Jeannie doesn't have to sell that camper."

"What do you mean?" I was a little taken aback. How did she know what Jeannie did or did not have to do?

"Listen. I also believe in you. I believe one hundred percent in your work too. I know you're talking to God or somebody. I'll loan you the money you need, in full." She said it so nonchalantly.

"You'll what?" I asked, stunned. I wasn't sure if I had heard that right.

"You heard me. I'll give you what you need. I know you're good for it. I trust you. I want every penny back, but I know you'll pay me." Kim's eyes glinted under her small-framed glasses. Then she broke out in a brilliant smile and started to laugh. I was sure it was the look on my face that gave her the chuckle.

My mouth literally hung open. I was astounded by what she had said. Never would I have expected even one person to help. Now I had two people offering to give me thousands of dollars to make these cards. The power of the Universe amazed me.

So began the monumental task of creating a deck of cards. I spent weeks researching every aspect of making them. From the design, card size, and printing to distribution, shipping, and marketing, I tapped every resource I could find. I visited nearly every metaphysical store I could get to within a one-day drive so I could look at other decks. I was now serious about what I wanted to do, and I wasn't going to jump in until I had my head fully wrapped around every step of the process. This was by far the most tedious part of the adventure.

The deck itself was much easier. My print date had been set, and I was now working under a deadline. My Spirit assistants aided me in choosing the fractal images. From there, I used my intuition to tune into the meaning of the image, which became the written blurb for the card. I was nearly exhausted and running out of time, so I had two friends help me with some of the meanings. Once I had all my materials together, I now had to make the files for the printer. This meant learning how to use another graphic design program that was foreign to me. It took a couple of days to learn the basics, thanks again to Google. Finally, exhausted, I had my deck completed, and everything was ready to go to print. It would take two and a half months before the cards arrived.

In the meantime, I was still doing websites and soul portraits. The only problem was that I wasn't charging much for either of them. Most of the time I built the sites either at a reduced rate or accepted barter as a form of payment. Most of my clients were holistic practitioners who didn't earn much, and I had a lot of compassion for them. I knew what it was like to not have money and I wanted to help everyone. Brent, however, had a different point of view, and he wasn't pleased with how I was running my business. I was working up to twelve hours a day and I had very little money to show for it.

With the increasing financial pressure on us, our relationship was feeling the crunch. Brent had had enough. During one of our now regular little spats, he finally put into words what had been bothering him for well over a year now.

"Cheryl, just what the hell is it you're trying to do here?" he asked me as we stood arguing in the middle of the living room.

"What are you talking about?"

"You work ten to twelve hours a day, every single day, and you have almost nothing to show for it! All you do is work." He rarely became angry like this. It took a lot for him to take a stand about anything, but he just couldn't hold it any longer. "You give it away to everyone...*everyone.* It's ridiculous! Look at what you've made in the last year."

"What? Brent, this conversation is ridiculous." I knew where it was headed and I didn't want to go there.

"In the last year," he sputtered, "you haven't even made ten thousand dollars—you've made less. You're always telling people you'll give them a break on the cost and then you work your ass off. You're doing graphic design, for Christ's sake! Most of those guys make at least forty, fifty thousand a year. But you aren't because you're giving it all away!"

"Yes, okay, that's true. But people *do* need help and if I can help them, then I will. Why do you have such a problem with that? I think you're just jealous because I'm doing something I really love to do and you're doing something you hate. You better look in your own backyard first, buddy, before you point over here to me!" My voice was getting louder and my defenses were raised. I knew I wasn't being logical, but I couldn't stop myself.

"You think that's what this is about? Well, it's *not*! It's about *you*. You act like a goddamn saint, Cheryl. It's like you're always trying to prove to the world that you're good enough. You need to look at your own self-worth."

Oh, that stung. He was right. I did have to look at that. But I was so pissed off with him by then that I wasn't about to admit he was right. I was also frustrated with myself. It seemed that no matter how much I worked on myself, there was always something else to look at. I was familiar with the analogy of personal growth work being like an onion. You could work on your stuff and do your healing, but there was always another, more tender layer underneath. The deeper you go, the more tears you needed to shed.

I was pissed off at the onion. I was pissed off at Brent. All I wanted to do was participate in the world and work in a different way from the current business model. I wanted to work with integrity, heart, and compassion. But my beliefs around my own self-worth were preventing me from working the new model in a healthy way. I knew it was something I was going to have to address.

One of the happiest days I experienced was the day a truck delivered three thousand decks of Path of the Soul Destiny Cards to my door. I opened one of the boxes and held a deck in my hand. I had never accomplished anything like this before and the tears started to flow. *You did it Cheryl, you really did it.* I held the deck to my chest as the reality of it sunk in. Finally, I had done something meaningful and important in my life. I had left a loving footprint on the world. I felt much gratitude to the Universe for helping me get past myself to actually accomplish this.

I had already started my marketing long before the decks arrived. Between what my two distributors ordered and what I had sold through pre-orders, I was sold out in less than four weeks. Never in my wildest dreams had I thought I'd even get the first batch sold within a year, let alone in a month! Now I had the money to order more and start paying Kim back. However, that took every penny of profit there was.

At the time, I wasn't really aware of how I was hiding behind my work. All my marketing and everything I did was about the work and the fractals, not about me. I pushed them out to the forefront while I remained hidden in the background. I liked it that way. It felt safe to me, and I certainly didn't see a problem with it.

Now that the cards were getting distributed, I accepted an invitation from Patty to attend an event at her store. I was growing more used to being around larger groups of people. I just couldn't do it often or for extended periods of time. I was like a turtle—I'd pop my head out of my shell when necessary to do what was required of me. Then right back in I'd go, tucked safely away from the world.

A good number of people attended the celebration, and I was very busy that day. I went back and forth between the store and the healing center next door. I had just come flying into the store to grab one of my art prints when I saw a shining face next to the counter. The woman looked to be about my age with long, thick brown hair. She was quite pretty with a youthful, childlike energy about her. Surprisingly, she stood at about my height too, perhaps an inch or two taller. Few people were as short as me, which is why I noticed her right away.

I beelined past her, on a mission to get my print. We made eye contact and I sent out a warm smile as I passed. On my way back to the door, she purposely stepped into my path so I would have to stop and talk with her.

"Hi. I'm Tracey Smith," she said. She was bubbly and all smiles as she introduced herself. "You're Cheryl Harnish, right?"

"Yes, I am." I returned a smile but I couldn't match the friendliness she exuded.

"Well, hey! Nice to meet you! I'm going to be doing readings here at the store, and I thought it would be nice to introduce myself."

She began to talk about her intuitive work and angel readings while I stood listening and watching in amazement. She was so exuberant—an obvious "people person." I found her fairylike. Her energy was light and airy, shimmery and youthful. She could certainly talk. I wondered what it would be like to be so personable and outgoing.

As she finished telling me about some of the volunteer work she had done, I excused myself as politely as I could and explained that I had someone waiting for me next door who wanted to see the art print I now held in my hand.

"Oh, go, go...you've got work to do. That's okay!" Her eyes danced and her smile beamed. "I'm sure we'll see each other lots now that I'm reading out of here."

"Oh, I'm sure we will!" I smiled and headed for the door.

I had no idea I had just met the person who would become one of my very best friends. No matter how much I wanted to segregate myself from the world, I was going to need the nurturing, feminine support only a really good girlfriend could provide. I also had no clue what was coming just around the bend and how much I was going to lean on both Tracey and Jeannie during what would become one of the toughest trials in my life.

For now it was life as normal. Receiving that little wake-up call from Brent about my self-worth did cause me to put a higher value on the work I was doing. It wasn't a lot, but it was enough. I felt I had at least addressed the issue somewhat. I started charging more for the soul portraits, which helped the process feel more in balance with the amount of work it took to make one.

I would use a person's name to connect into their energy while I meditated, then I would quietly head to the computer, where I would receive guidance about what formulas to apply to their fractal. For a couple of hours each day I would work on it. Most of the personal fractals took about three weeks to complete. I'd know it was finished when I felt a familiar resonating gong in the back of my head and down my spine.

One of the biggest lessons I learned about sharing the intuitive information I received was from doing these soul portraits. I had started one for a woman whom I'll call Doris. Right from the start, nearly every second image that rendered during the making of her fractal contained symbols related to the female reproductive organs. I was seeing ovaries—sometimes one and other times four or five. I'd also see the whole uterus every so often. It was just the strangest thing. When the final image rendered, my inner gong alerted me her fractal was complete. I could see no trace of the ovaries or uterus that had been dominating her fractal earlier.

At this time, I still called people on the phone to give them the reading on their fractal after it was finished. I would send them an art print of their portrait for framing and then call them to share the intuitive information from the image. Before I began the work, it was easier to have people e-mail me their information. I'd avoid talking to them whenever possible; that way I would know little about them. I felt I could pick up too much on a person if I spoke with them before I did their fractal. The less my thinking mind knew, the less control and interference it had over the intuitive process.

Before I dialed Doris's phone number, I had a small battle with myself. The doubter within me began to speak. *Cheryl, you cannot mention anything about those ovaries to her. It is utterly ridiculous and she'll think you've lost it, for sure.* My fear of being wrong and not being clear in my intuition was trying to hold me back. But I knew better than to listen to that voice. *Not a chance, girl. You tell her exactly what you saw and nothing less. If it's completely crazy, then that's Spirit's fault, not yours.*

I sucked in a breath and dialed the phone. A friendly voice of a woman in about her mid-fifties answered. I gave her the breakdown of what was in the image. I told her what I was getting from the colors and layout, everything that could be seen with the eye. Then it was either time to hang up or time to cough it up. I rolled my eyes at both myself and my Guides for putting me in this position.

"Ah, Doris?" I said. "Now, there's one more thing with your fractal."

"Oh really! What is it?" She had been enthralled with the reading and was happy to hear more.

"Well, okay...now, this may sound a bit strange, and I don't really want to tell you, but since I saw it, I have to share it." I heard her make a sound of acknowledgment and I had to force myself to continue. "I don't know why, Doris, but the entire time I was making your fractal, all I saw were ovaries and a uterus. Over and over they showed up, the whole time. But then, in the final fractal I sent you, there was not a trace of them. I don't know why." I did want to defend myself and what I had seen. But I stopped talking and awaited her response.

"Really?" she said and started laughing. At first I thought she was laughing at me, and I started to cringe in my chair. But then she continued, "Yeah, my body is still totally pissed at me for having a hysterectomy ten years ago!"

I looked up to my Guides, then hung my head down in shame. Reflexively, my hand slapped my forehead. *A hysterectomy? A hysterectomy! Of course!* It made perfect sense...now I knew. I was once again amazed at how they worked. Why the hell did I keep doubting them and myself? This was really going to have to stop.

Needless to say, most people were very pleased with their fractal, and they loved the reading that accompanied it. Word was spreading everywhere. I was so excited when I received my first request for a soul portrait from outside North America. It was a small "woo-hoo" moment for me. My work was really getting out there.

The hysterectomy fractal experience, however, paled in comparison to the experience I had while making the personal fractal for a woman named Kristina Stolz from Sweden.

I had been working on Kristina's fractal for a couple of weeks and I felt it was nearing completion. Some of the colors coming through the images were magnificent, looking almost metallic. I had done only one or two other personal fractals that had developed this look. I found I was enjoying the feeling of working in her energy even more than usual.

Often when I was deeply involved in making a fractal, I would experience little bits of strange phenomenon. I'd see sparkles glitter out of the corner of my eyes, or wisps of something moving behind me in the reflection of my monitor, or voices and sounds I knew were not really there. Very often I'd get the sensation of a gentle breeze blowing past my face or that one or two of my hairs on the top of my head were being caressed. It had become so common that none of it fazed me anymore. It was as though I was halfway between this physical realm and the spiritual. And I honestly enjoyed being there.

Today, working on Kristina's fractal was like any other day. I applied the formulas and waited for the images to render. I was completely focused and deep into what I was doing when suddenly I distinctly felt a hand on each of my shoulders. It wasn't merely a brushing sensation or tingle. I physically felt two people standing behind me, and simultaneously they each put a hand on my shoulders.

Instantly, my attention was sucked back into the physical world. I screamed from the sheer shock of it, as if they had said "boo" to me instead. Frightened, I sprang out of my office chair, which sent it rolling backward across the kitchen floor. It seemed as if that chair was always rolling away and I was always jumping around, freaking out at my computer.

"Oh no...no, no, *no!*" I yelled as I tried to wipe my shoulders clean of the lingering memory of the touch. "For God's sake, you guys...nobody touches me! Do you understand? Don't *ever* freakin' touch me!"

I was angry because I felt as though my physical boundaries had been crossed. It was the same feeling a woman might have if an uninvited stranger patted her bottom. I felt invaded and violated. I spun around in a little circle, intermittently wiping my upper body off, then making fists at the creepy feelings. "God damn it!" I whined, releasing a long string of my favorite profanities. It took a good three or four minutes of drama before I got it out of my system.

Once the heebie-jeebies were gone, I walked across the kitchen to retrieve my chair. *What the hell...I mean really!* I was half talking to them and half talking to myself. I sighed in frustration with both myself and the Guides as I rolled the chair back over to my desk. I needed to sit down.

All right, Cheryl, think about this for a minute. Do you remember what you have to do here? You have to stop reacting, stop allowing your mind to tell you what is what, then tune into those two and see what they're about. I was pleased that I had appeared to have learned the lesson from the alien fractal experience. With my more rational self now in control, I set out to connect with the two overly touchy-feely Beings so I could find out exactly who and what they were.

I wiggled myself into the chair to get a little more comfortable and then closed my eyes. It took only seconds to connect with them. I couldn't see anything in my mind's eye, nor could I hear anything. My intuition was running on feelings. I easily distinguished that one felt more feminine and one felt more masculine in nature. Between the two of them, I had a strong feeling that they were almost like a mother and father. While they didn't feel like Kristina's parents, they did somehow belong to her. I continued to feel their loving and nurturing energy, but I couldn't figure out who they were.

Since I wasn't able to pick up anything more than that, I took the time to ground and focus myself. Once I felt connected to Kristina again, I opened my eyes and pulled myself back to my desk. I sat there, hand on the mouse, waiting for direction. Once I finally felt the pull toward a formula, I entered it and watched the image form in front of my eyes.

I was stunned at what had now revealed itself on my screen. Still keeping to the theme of metallic colors, within the vibrant golden yellow in the middle of the fractal were two faces. One was female, the other was male. There in front of me appeared what I understood to be the faces of the two beings that had just physically touched me. As I sat there, the resonating vibration of the gong ran down my back. This was her completed fractal.

Nothing remotely close to this had ever happened before. Other beings had appeared in the fractals, yes, but never had they given me a physical, real-world indication they were actually present. Not an ounce of skepticism or doubt entered my mind. I was so moved by both the experience itself and seeing their faces that my eyes began to water. It was an incredible feeling. I simply sat there for the longest time, looking at the image on the screen as the tears rolled down my cheeks.

Once I pulled myself together, I felt I had to call Kristina immediately. I looked up her information and began dialing her number. This time I had no fear about sharing what had happened or what I'd picked up intuitively. Moments later, I was greeted in Swedish by a female voice.

"This is Kristina," said the woman, now speaking in English in a thick accent.

"Kristina, this is Cheryl Harnish. I'm calling you about your soul portrait. Do you have a few minutes to talk?" As I waited for her reply, I hit the send button on the e-mail that contained a picture of her fractal.

"Well, absolutely I do." She waited for me to continue.

"I just finished making your fractal a few minutes ago and it was one of the most incredible experiences I have ever had."

"Why? What happened?" Her voice indicated concern.

Wanting to reassure her, I answered, "Oh, nothing bad, no, no. It was good, actually. I mean...I had two people show up...in person, it seemed." And I explained the whole story of what had happened only moments earlier.

"Oh my God," she answered. She too was apparently shocked and didn't know what to say.

"Open your e-mail and you can see what showed up." I waited as she went to her computer and opened the attachment. I knew the moment she had it opened because I heard her reaction. She took a large inward breath. While she gathered her thoughts, I continued to speak. "They showed up in your fractal, Kristina. Those are the two. Your parents haven't passed over, have they?"

There was nothing but quiet sobs on the other end of line. Out of respect, I waited for her reply. "No, God no. My parents are alive and well." Then she broke into heavier sobs. Between the weeping and her heavy accent I had to listen carefully to make out what she was saying. "I have been sad for a couple of months now, and I have been praying to my Guides night after night. I told them I need to know they are with me. I need to know who they are and that they are really with me. This world is so hard sometimes. Then by like a miracle or something, I don't know what, I came across your website. And it was strange how your website ended up on my computer, but I believe everything happens for a reason. I was just trusting the process. So I said to Spirit, 'Okay, this is what you want me to do—all right, I will do it.' I didn't have the money for this but I did it anyway. And now look at them. They are here. They are really with me."

Understanding all too well that indescribable feeling of knowing that Spirit is truly with you and loves you, I too began to cry. For a few minutes neither one of us spoke—we were simply overwhelmed with this incredible experience.

We ended up talking for well over an hour that day. Kristina, I discovered, was highly connected with her intuitive side, and there were a couple of things she said that took me by surprise. I knew it was a sign that she was going to be an important person in my life. And I was right.

We talked regularly on the phone and within a few months she had singlehandedly arranged a couple of talks and workshops for me throughout Southern Sweden. Although I didn't have a penny to my name and everything was tied up in the cards, I did have a credit card. My heart told me to go and I had to follow that. Trusting that everything would work out financially, I made my way to Scandinavia.

As Spirit would have it, I earned just enough money to pay for my trip with a little left over to allow for three days of playtime in England with Kristina. When we arrived at Gatwick airport just outside of London, we had only one plan. We would let Spirit guide us to where we needed to go.

Inside the airport, we approached the window to purchase our train tickets. I said to the teller, "Well, we want to see England and we have three days. Give me two tickets to wherever you think we should go." He slid the tickets under the glass partition and I happily announced our destination to Kristina. "Looks like we're going to Bath!"

I had no idea where Bath was. Since I had either been absent or stoned while I was in school, I didn't receive much of an education in geography. It wasn't a required credit when I went back to school years later, so I skipped it.

Bath was one of the most incredible places I had ever seen. It was rich with history and visually stunning. Remnants of Roman rule were everywhere. This little city was filled with exquisite architecture and of course the underground hot springs that the Romans had turned into bath houses, giving the city its name.

We were also only a short bus trip away from Stonehenge, as well as a small town called Glastonbury. We visited both places, but Glastonbury held much more for me energetically than Stonehenge. The main street of this small town was lined end to end with alternative stores of every flavor, from Pagan and Wiccan to angelic and new age. At the center of the town lay the ruins of King Arthur's castle. We ended up at the Chalice Well, a short walk from the town's center, which was said to contain healing waters. Traces of the Knights Templar could be seen throughout the gardens that were planted to honor the well.

I don't know what it was about the gardens and the well, but from the moment I walked in I was overwhelmed with an irrepressible urge to cry. I found a private spot on a bench, where I sat and wept for nearly half an hour. By the time Kristina came to check on me, I had finished my release. I learned many deep and personal things about myself during the short time I spent in the energy of this extremely powerful place.

In order to exit the gardens, we had to walk through the shop. I stood outside begging Kristina to take the only deck of cards I had left. I wanted her to show the manager of the shop to see if they would be interested in carrying them.

"I'm not doing that for you! No way! That's your job," she retorted. "Now you go. Get. Go in there and ask them. You just sat out here for half the day crying about how you won't allow yourself to be fully empowered, and yet here you stand asking me to do this? Oh, you're crazy all right. I'm not doing it! Now get in there and get empowered."

I wanted to sulk. Despite my efforts at growth and change, I still had a problem talking about my work, the cards, the fractals. It was ridiculous. It felt as if I was pitching my work and I didn't want to have to do that. Since the only way out was through that shop, I had to follow Kristina in.

We looked around the tiny store for about ten minutes. That's when Kristina whispered behind me in a firm tone, "Go now—do it now." She gently nudged my shoulder, forcing me to take a step forward to keep my balance. "That's right. There you go."

I threw Kristina a dirty look and then swallowed the lump in my throat, pushing it down to my stomach. I think I called her a name or two in the privacy of my mind. She was like a mama bird pushing the baby out of the nest, loving but tough. I took a couple more steps to the counter and asked the girl who I could show my cards to. My lips and hands were shaking with nerves. I was embarrassed that my body was telling everyone how I really felt.

I handed the manager the deck and filled out a small piece of paper with my information. She said she didn't have time right now, but she'd look at them later. My writing looked like a five-year-old's because of my nervous shakes.

Back at home two weeks later, the Chalice Well contacted me, saying how much they loved the cards. I was completely lovestruck with England and vowed I would return again. I was also in love with the people of Sweden and was delighted to have met so many wonderful people. I didn't know that I would end up returning to Sweden in very a short time and that it was secretly holding one of the deepest reawakenings of my life.

～❦～ *11* ～❦～

The Hardest Part of Life is Change

They say everything happens for a reason. Most of the time, I believe in that. I had a hard time deciphering the meaning or reasons for my broken-down marriage, though. On my return from Sweden it had become painfully clear that what I had once shared with Brent was gone—nothing was left except dreamy memories of days past. I had always felt he was my soul mate and I believed that even still. The pain of what our marriage had become made that belief even harder to deal with. To me he was now nothing more than a ghost of the man I had married. Eventually, I knew there was nothing left for me to do; I had tried everything I knew, but we seemed unable to put things back together. I couldn't live like this anymore. I was an all-or-nothing kind of girl. I needed passion, connection, communication, spiritual companionship, and someone who was willing to do their own inner work, for themselves and in the relationship. I'd had that with him once, but it was gone now. I didn't even know this man anymore.

I fell into conflict within myself. My heart was squelched and bleeding, yet my head insisted I should stay—for all the wrong reasons. Stay for the boys, stay for the family, stay because it's safe, stay because you can't support yourself, stay because this is who you are, and many more reasons that seemed so convincing at the time. This was probably the first time in my life that I didn't immediately jump to the calling of my heart, and I was going to pay for it in a very big way.

Unable to face what my life with Brent had become, I used the rest of my life to create a distraction. I was so busy now between tending my two boys and the websites, card promotion, and personal fractals I barely had time to breathe, and frankly, that's how I wanted it. Meditation was once a faithful and daily routine. Now, I did it when I had the time, which wasn't often. It hurt too much to breathe deeply into a broken heart. How could I attempt to open the one place I was trying hard to close off so I could function above the pain on a daily basis? How could I connect into love with my Guides when the love in my physical life had withered away? I hadn't heard the voices of my Guides since I had published the deck, so I rationalized that I wasn't missing much by not meditating anyway.

After many months of this, I became bitter and angry. I often awoke in the middle of the night, only to hide in the bathroom to cry. I had a hard time being nice to anyone. I was oozing with dark emotions that I was consciously stuffing away. My inner trash had built up and it was overflowing everywhere I looked. It was no surprise either when the depression set in.

I would sit in the living room, just staring, in a numbed-out state. I was having an extremely hard time concentrating or focusing on anything, and my work was suffering. It was a familiar side effect caused by the depression. I had effectively shut down.

I stared at the pine-paneled wall and white trim that lent to the country cabin look of the old farmhouse. My eyes glanced over at the large-screen TV that had taken us a year to save for. There wasn't much in our house besides the basics, but it was still a cute place. I looked up at the stucco ceiling and, just like cloud gazing, I looked for shapes of things I might recognize. It was the large black crack that captured my attention. This crack started at one end of the house and ran all the way along the length of the house to the other end. Years of strain on a feeble foundation had found its weak point, where the ceiling met the wall. Year after year the crack had grown along the crevice until it reached the other end. Now, there was nowhere left for the crack to go. We'd had the farm's carpenter come and inspect it, but he'd said there was nothing they could do. They would have to tear the entire house down and start from scratch, which they weren't going to do. Eventually, the wall was just going to fall in and the house would crumble. It was just like our marriage. Our foundation was gone, there were cracks everywhere, and it was beyond repair. It was caving in and crushing me and I was slowly dying. I knew without a doubt that it was time for me to go. I had to make an escape plan and begin evacuation as soon as possible.

It was the hardest thing I have ever had to do in my life. I had to walk away from my family and from the life I had spent years creating. I had to step out into the world alone and it was scary.

Above all, there were my children to consider. Jaden and Brent were like Batman and Robin—they were a team, a duo, and I couldn't separate them. We knew Jaden would be better served if his life remained somewhat familiar too. Ripping him away from his home, his school, and his friends was certainly not in his best interest. I made plans to move out with Brandon, who was now nineteen. He was working full time and would be helping with the rent.

For the first three months, Brandon and I shared a small but cute apartment in the main part of town, only fifteen minutes away from the farm. For nearly the entire three months, I cried. I found the night to be the hardest, when I would crawl into bed alone. I thought some nights the pain might actually suffocate me and kill me, it hurt that much. I tried to hold myself together as best I could by doing the only thing I could. I worked. Since my office was in my home, it was easy to work fourteen to sixteen-hour days. I worked until my eyes bled, in hopes of numbing my brain.

I had chosen the first available apartment I could find, instead of following my feelings. My building stood on the busiest corner of our small city. Traffic and buses created a constant droning. My patio sat directly above it all. I cringed every time I went out there, feeling as though I was on display for the public below. I dreamed daily about having a house, quiet and private with an ocean view, but I knew that would cost me a small fortune in rent each month, so all I could do was keep dreaming.

Jeannie and Tracey became my pillars of strength. They had literally picked my face up out of the mud, cleaned me off, and helped me to get moving forward. I had never bonded with other women like that before; years of street life had taught me to trust no one. But I was older now, more healed, and desperately in need. These two were real women, empowered and strong. They were solid and present. Both of them had been through a divorce themselves. They knew my pain and it created a bond between us. They had more than earned my trust with their unrelenting support and I loved them.

It was early spring now and I was at home, continuing to bury myself in work. I wasn't at all recovered, but at least I didn't cry at night anymore. I was also starting to feel the whispers of self-esteem returning, and I looked forward to my time with my girlfriends. When I saw Jeannie's number come up on the call display of the phone, I answered right away.

"Hello, goofy!" greeted the voice on the other end. I had no idea why she had taken to calling me that, but it was meant in an endearing way, and I liked it.

"What's up, girly?" I asked.

"I'm so excited! I just got the keys to my new place, and I thought maybe you'd like to come for a drive and take a look."

I began to chuckle. "Absolutely! I'll be waiting for you down at the front doors."

As soon as I was in the car, she began to share every detail of the new house. Her energy was so high it was contagious. Her new place was only a few minutes from mine, and by the time she parked the car I was giddy with excitement too.

Her house was the second one in from the corner, but she had parked her car on the side street and we now stood at the driveway of the house directly on the corner, next to her place.

"Okay, we're going in this way." She pointed and her feet began moving forward.

"What?" I said, hurrying to catch up with her. "We're cutting across the neighbor's yard? No, let's walk around on the sidewalk." I didn't like the thought of trespassing like that.

"No, it's okay," she assured me. "This place also belongs to the company I'm renting from. Don't worry, it's empty. They bought these three properties, and they're going to sell the lots to a developer. They don't know how long I'll get to stay here, but they figure I'd have at least six months to a year before they sell."

I looked at the towering house beside Jeannie's as we passed. It was unique. Covering nearly half of the front of the house was the largest wisteria vine I had ever seen. Huge purple blossoms that looked like bunches of grapes covered most of the greenery. It was stunning to behold and the smell was intoxicating. The entire property was enclosed by tall trees and bushes. Without sneaking in as we had done, no one could have seen into the private yard.

"Well, you're going to have to start going the other way around when the new tenants move in here because I don't think they'd want you making a trail on their lawn," I warned.

"I don't have to worry about that. They aren't going to be renting it out."

By now we had come to the other side of the property. There, the trees had been cut and trained over the years to form an archway. It was somewhat overgrown now, and we had to force our way through the thin branches that resisted our passing.

We popped out on the other side where a lovely little sixties-style home greeted us. This yard was just as lush with plants and trees as the first house, and both of them were completely overgrown. The inside of the house had been updated here and there over the years and it had a welcoming feel. I felt so much joy for Jeannie as she gave me the tour.

Following the same pathway, we headed back to the car. As we cleared the archway, I was once again taken by the smell and view of the wisteria and it led to an obvious question.

"Jeannie? How come they aren't going to rent this place?"

"The landlord said the inside is in rough shape and they can't rent it. They don't want to put up the money to fix it up."

Curiosity got the best of me and I headed up the stairs to the glass front door to take a peek inside. I cupped my hands around my eyes and planted my nose on the glass. First I noticed the dark wood floors in the hallway that led to the bedrooms. When I shifted my eyes to the stairway leading up to the second level, my eyes grew wide and I gasped out loud.

"Oh my God, Jeannie! The stairs are covered with custom tiles and all the floors are wood. What in the world could be so wrong with the place? I love it!" I had just been swept off my feet. The house was extraordinary and had a great energy about it. I was mesmerized by it. "Jeannie, can you imagine if I lived right next door to you? How awesome would that be?" I looked up into my friend's face.

Jeannie was enthusiastic about the idea. When she got home later, she spoke with the landlord. With a little persuading, he was willing to at least show me the place. My love became mingled with disgust once I got a good look inside the hippie house, as I now called it.

None of the upstairs level had any baseboards or crown

moldings on the walls, which left the insulation and plastic exposed. Half of the stone fireplace was stripped of drywall. Everywhere I looked, the small gap left between the walls and wood flooring was filled with balls of rabbit excrement. Unappealing crayon and marker decorated many of the walls. Upstairs were the kitchen, dining room, and living room. Windows lined every wall. From there, the eye could travel outward to an almost mystical view of the mountains surrounded by ocean. The patio was almost completely private, with only one or two small spots where passersby might be able to steal a look.

Though I was repelled by the filth and crayon graffiti, my heart was screaming at me to take action now. I had to live here. Brent and I had remodeled half of the old farmhouse, so I'd had experience in fixing up a place.

"I'll take it. How much?" I asked the property manager.

"Well, I don't know. We weren't even going to rent this place. And you know we aren't going to put a penny into it, right? You'd be on your own with the expenses."

My answer was quick. "Understood."

"Well, make me an offer."

If I was going to live here, it had to be cheap. I was tired of living with Brandon. He was a typical teenager, always partying. He would be more than happy to change our arrangement so he didn't have to listen to his nagging mother anymore. I was going to need to rent at a price I could pay on my own, and it wasn't much. I took a big breath and tossed out my offer. Any house of this size with a view, a full front and back yard, apple, plum, and cherry trees, four bedrooms, an office, a den, a half-finished basement, fireplaces in the living room and master bedroom, and a one hundred and eighty degree view of the ocean and mountains would cost, at minimum, three thousand dollars a month. What I now offered the manager was nearly a joke.

Without hesitating, he answered, "All right, we'll take it. I'll get the paperwork ready and we'll meet tomorrow."

I could scarcely believe it. This was exactly what I had been wanting and somehow I had manifested my dream. I was delirious with both joy and gratitude for the gift I had received. I knew this was the place I could start to put my broken life back together.

Brent was not as excited about my new place, to say the least. This only meant more work for him. We had remained friends throughout our separation. For one, it was important to both of us for Jaden to see and learn that people could get along if they worked at it. Secondly, we actually were friends. We loved each other very much, we just no longer knew how to make that love work in a relationship with each other.

Between me, Brent, and a few volunteers, the place was fixed up to a livable condition in a very short time and under my allotted budget. The main level of the house sparkled now and most people would exclaim in pleasure when they saw it. At last, I felt settled.

By mid-summer I felt as though I had found a bit of flow in my life. I had stopped doing any work that called on my intuition. Even though I had an ever-growing list of people waiting for a soul portrait, I couldn't do it. I wasn't healed enough inside. Even the energy thing had vanished, which told me my heart wasn't open in the way it needed to be in order to do the work. It was a matter of integrity. Instead, I focused on websites and helping people whenever I could. I would help set up and promote talks for people, of course at no charge. I designed an absurd number of websites, nearly half of them either at an extremely reduced rate or free. I just couldn't stop myself from helping someone if I knew I could.

I was excited the day I received a call from Jim Law. We had been introduced by a mutual friend, Allison. Jim lived in Sedona, Arizona, and was co-founder of a production and video company. His partner wanted to interview me for a film he was working on. Jim very kindly offered me a room at his place while I was there. He knew I was on a limited budget. I would be staying for two weeks, even though we were only filming one day. I was ecstatic about going to Sedona, not to mention being interviewed.

I fell in love with Arizona from the moment I stepped off the plane. I had never felt heat like that before. The moment I walked out of the airport's automatic doors, the heat smacked me in the face, and my knees nearly buckled as I made my way into the parking lot. I felt as though I was standing in the middle of a forest fire as invisible flames licked at my skin. I didn't care, though—I loved the heat and the beauty of the arid landscape. Sedona was in the high mountain desert, an hour and half drive north of Phoenix. It was a couple degrees cooler, thank God. I lived in the north, near the ocean, and I had only ever experienced the moderately cool climate native to Canada, but within a couple of days my body had adjusted and I didn't want to think about going back to the damp cold again.

Jim was a big, good-looking guy, standing over six foot one. His hair had naturally lightened to a dark sandy blonde from the nonstop sunlight. We joked and laughed and got along fine, but I was not interested in anything more than that. I suspected he might be attracted to me, but I wasn't sure. I was a bit daft when it came to that sort of thing. I made sure all of my conduct conveyed the message that I was happy to be single and planned to stay that way. The very last thing I wanted was another man in my life.

I was only beginning to regain a sense of myself. Being pregnant at seventeen had taken away the years most people spend growing up and exploring life, relationships, careers, and the world. Instead, I was at home, learning how to be the best mother I could be with the skills I had. I'd never had a time in my life where I had no label. I was either a mother or wife, but I'd never had the opportunity to be just me. I was beginning to enjoy my new freedom.

Jim was a courteous, friendly host and a knowledgeable tour guide. He took me to many of the places that were known to only the locals. We hiked the small mountains, visited ancient caves of the shamans, swam in remote private creeks, and of course, hung out at night at the premier spots known for UFO activity. I felt blessed to have my own private tour of some of the most powerful energy spots on the planet.

My first night there didn't turn out quite as I had hoped. Jim's house was an architectural marvel, with a large, spiraling staircase representing activated strands of DNA. Using sacred geometry as his guide, he had designed his round adobe-style home himself. Twin towers of solid amethyst greeted me when I entered the house. They were nearly twice my height and I was immediately taken with their beauty and energy. The main living quarters were upstairs, but he was using the room downstairs to sleep at night because it was cooler down there. I was given the luxurious master bedroom for my stay. The king-sized bed was adorned with Egyptian cotton sheets. The private patio led directly out to a secluded hot tub, and beyond that were hillside trails, all on Jim's private property. The ensuite bathroom was just as stunning with a large, tiled walk-in shower that could have easily fit a party of six. Beyond the shower was another room that held the toilet and bidet. Every inch of the house was immaculate. I had never before stayed in a place like this and I felt nervous. I didn't want to touch anything.

I should have slept on the floor that night. And I would have, had I known my period was going to sneak up and surprise me while I slept. When I awoke in the morning, I was appalled. *Oh dear God, please tell me I'm dreaming. Please! This cannot be real!* Of all places, it had to happen on the single most expensive bed I had ever slept on, with the most expensive and lavish sheets my body had ever touched. Worst of all, it belonged to a man! I leaped up out of bed with both hands between my legs. Thank God it was all tiled floor. I quickly cleaned myself up in the shower and took care of my business. The warm shower, however, did nothing to soothe the anxiety and nausea I felt when I returned to look at the bed. I quickly stripped the sheets from the bed, and my heart only sunk deeper when I saw the mattress below. What was once pristine and perfect was now permanently blemished by me. I cleaned out the sheets the best I could in the washroom sink. I balled up all the linen on the bed, strategically placing it over the soiled spot.

Since I was a very early riser, Jim had still not awakened. If there was ever a time to go smoke a cigarette, this was it. I sneaked out my door as quietly as I could and headed up one of the trails, where I could hide. Jim had disclosed, in one of our casual conversations, just how much he despised smoking. I was going to do my best to hide my nasty habit from him.

Even in the early hours of morning, it was hot. My flip-flops didn't offer much of a grip against the loose red rocks of the hillside, and it was hard to find a place to hide with only sparse juniper trees and low, small bushes. By the time I found a place out of view of the house, my heart was pounding and my legs were shaky. After a couple of years of mostly sitting in an office chair, my body was not up to the demands I had just put it through.

I sat up there for almost an hour. I was so upset that I didn't ever want to come back down. I wasn't quite finished my second smoke when I heard my name being called from below. My panic alarm rang in my head and I quickly put my cigarette out as if I was a naughty teenager caught by their parent. I waved my hands frantically as if that was somehow going to magically blow away the stink. I didn't want to go down and have to face Jim, but I did.

I made my way back down the hill as slowly as I could. I was trying to buy time so the odor wouldn't be as strong on me and give my secret away. Jim was waiting down at the house when I arrived.

"What are you doing out here so early in the morning?"

"Why are you out here looking for me?" I answered with a question so I wouldn't have to lie.

"You're my guest! I knocked on your door a couple of times and then I hollered for you. When you didn't answer, I stuck my head in to make sure you were okay. But when I looked in, I saw the bed all ripped apart and the patio door open! I thought you'd been abducted!" He had a genuine look of concern on his face.

Reluctantly, I explained what had happened in the night, and how I was so upset that I needed to go outside. It wasn't the full truth, but it wasn't a lie either. I got to keep my smoking a secret

for just a bit longer, until I was ready to tell him myself. And he wasn't upset about the bed at all, not like I thought he would be.

I think the rough start helped to break the ice between us, making the rest of the time a pleasure in comparison. Everything went smoothly until it came time for the interview.

Jim's partner was the one conducting the interview on film. It seemed to be doomed from the beginning. We were simply not on the same page, and I didn't understand any of his questions. Clearly, my lack of experience with interviews played a big part in that, but the fact that we couldn't relate to each other made it all the worse. I was disappointed with how it came out, but I was determined not to let it ruin my trip or to take away from the last five days I had in Arizona.

Later that day, Allison called to say she was coming down from Hopi to visit for a few days. Since we had only ever talked on the phone, I was excited to finally meet with her. I had no idea what I was really in for; I thought I was just going to meet a friend. Spirit, however, had other plans that were going to take me deep into the world of extraterrestrials and beyond, testing the limits of my newfound self-empowerment.

12

The Greatest Road Trip Ever

The next morning I awoke with anticipation, but Allison wasn't going to be arriving until late afternoon. Since I hadn't planned anything else for the day, I thought I would get a bit of sunshine in the morning, before it became too hot.

The patio off my room was nearly level with the earth. On it sat a four-foot-tall pyramid shape made from copper tubing, with a large quartz crystal resting on its tip. This object took up nearly half of the space on the deck. The idea was to sit inside it and meditate, but I wasn't interested in anything involving meditation this morning. I just wanted to enjoy the dry air and sunshine.

As I looked out at the landscape, I noticed some movement on the pathway. The sun was still low, which created long shadows down the hillside. I leaned out a little more. With my eyes squinted and a hand at my forehead to block out the bright light, I tried to get a better look.

I thought at first it might be a rat because that was about the size of it, but the movements didn't match. It certainly wasn't one of the hundreds of little lizards that I'd see everywhere I stepped.

They were much too small and they moved like little bullets across the dusty earth. Since I was unfamiliar with the wildlife of the high mountain desert, I decided to remain still and wait for it to get close enough. The creature was slowly heading toward me, and I didn't have to wait long.

Soon I had a clear view—and this was no rat! In a slow, graceful manner, one long hairy leg after another took a step forward. I have no idea why I didn't immediately scream. With a tarantula of that size walking straight toward the deck, I ought to have bolted like a madwoman into the house. I was certainly scared but not terrified; instead, my heart pounded as fascination gripped me. I just had to admire this beautiful creature that I had only ever seen on TV.

The most amazing thing about this enormous spider—almost the size of a dinner plate—was how smooth and elegant its movements were. It wasn't nearly as creepy as those little black spiders that crawled up the drain of the bathtub and lay in wait until I stepped into the shower. No, those little buggers were ghoulish and fast and always made me scream.

This mother of all spiders was more like a small animal than a creepy-crawly bug. And its grace mesmerized me. I wished desperately for a video camera to record it, but I didn't even own a camera. Then it occurred to me that Jim did! I bolted inside to tell him about the visitor, and he ran to get his camera and met me out on the deck.

By now, it was only two arm lengths away from me. Just a couple of well-spaced wooden slats of the deck was all that sat between me and this wondrous creature. I carefully angled the camera and got a couple of really great shots, which I emailed to Jaden right away. I knew he'd love them.

I wished I had brought Ted Andrews' book *Animal Speak* with me here. I knew a little of the meaning of spider medicine, how it was the weaver of the alphabet, but that's all I could recall. In just a few days, however, I would learn exactly why grandmother spider, in all her glory and grace, had come to see me.

For the rest of the day, I hung out and waited for Allison's arrival. I did a small hike on Cathedral Rock, which was just a ten-minute walk from the house. Thankfully, Allison showed up earlier than planned and saved me from my boredom. Once she arrived, my time in Sedona was anything but boring.

Allison was taller than me, but who wasn't? Her bouncy, short black hair lent to her deceptively youthful appearance. She had a very strong personality, but I was able to see past that. I could see clearly that this woman had a good heart. For so many of my younger years, I too had some rough edges that most people couldn't get past. I naturally repelled people, even though I didn't consciously mean to. It had taken a great deal of healing and growth work to change that in myself, so I had compassion when I saw it in her.

With the arrival of my new friend, Jim was now released of his duty to entertain and accompany me. He had plenty of work to do and was gone most of the time. Of all the small gifts of learning that Allison provided me, the biggest one she offered was a chance to capture a piece of my personal freedom.

We were lying out by the hot tub, trying to get some sun. It was so hot that we spent most of our time under the cool, refreshing spray of the outdoor shower rather than on our towels tanning.

"Listen, I'm going to take my top off because I'd like to get rid of some of these tan lines," Allison said. "Hope you're okay with that?"

I was an easygoing person in that way. I wasn't bothered by what anyone did, as long as it made them happy. "Oh yeah, I don't care. It just won't be me lying here with my boobs hanging out!"

"What? Why wouldn't you, Cheryl? No one can see us here! It doesn't get better than this!"

I took a big breath. I just didn't do things like that. Certainly you could say I was reserved, but there was something much deeper to it. If I did take off my top, then I would be exposed and seen, in a symbolic way, and it made me so uncomfortable that I just couldn't handle the thought of it. I knew it was only my ego creating the resistance, so I carefully explained all the reasons that prevented me from doing it. Essentially, I had to call myself out on my stuff, if I wanted to get past it.

Allison listened intently until I was finished, then stood up without saying anything. She looked me straight in the eye and flung off her bikini top dramatically.

Bouncing and dancing around in a circle, she hollered, "There! I did it! I'm free, I'm free, I'm free!"

I sat on the side of the hot tub, laughing at her craziness. I loved it!

Suddenly she turned serious. "All right, your turn." She stood still for a moment.

"Oh...I just can't. You know, I..."

"Do it, Cheryl. Just stand the hell up and *do it*!" She was smiling and playful, but she really meant it.

I wondered how I always ended up with these strong, bossy women who always made me do something I didn't want to do. I knew she was right, though. And deep inside I was grateful for the opening she had provided, to help me get past my own self.

I leaped up and got that top off me as fast as possible, before I had time to change my mind.

"Woo-hoo!" Allison bellowed as she began to dance in a circle again, her face tilted up to the sky.

I did the same. A wash of tears ran down my face. I hadn't just taken my top off, I had also removed years of shame and hiding. I had just flung away years of not being good enough and needing to remain small. I now stood bare and exposed to God and the world, my arms outstretched and my face up to the sun, smiling widely. It was the greatest feeling of freedom I had ever experienced. It was freedom from myself, and it was glorious!

That evening, Allison and I headed out to an important event for her—the reason she had come to Sedona in the first place. She planned to connect with a Mayan priest who was visiting. She had an important agenda and speaking to this man was a part of it. We stayed for almost two hours after the event was finished, Allison doing enough talking for both of us. In my usual fashion, I didn't say a word.

She arranged to meet with Juan, the priest, at the local coffee shop the next day at one o'clock. She invited me along, I supposed, because I had been there the previous evening. We sat at the table for what seemed like forever. He was very late, and we were nearly ready to leave when he finally arrived.

Juan and his son sat at the table with me and Allison. Again, she did most of the talking. The man spoke very little English and his accent was so thick at times it was difficult to understand him. When he started to talk about love and fire in the heart, something I could relate to, I became a full participant in the conversation.

For over an hour we sat around the table and talked. As though I had been sucked into a vortex, I became completely unaware of anything around us. No people, no noise or bustle—there was nothing except us, connecting deeply from our hearts.

It wasn't until Juan's assistant came to retrieve him that we pulled ourselves back to the here and now. Our goodbyes were very emotional; all of us had tears in our eyes. We'd each been touched by the presence of the others in a deep and meaningful way.

I had only two days left now before it was time to return home. Allison and I were having a blast, and she didn't want the fun to end either. That's when she came up with a plan.

"Cheryl, I know what we're going to do," she said excitedly as we sat on the royal bed. "You and I are going to drive up to the Hopi reservation and spend the night. The next day we'll travel up to the border by New Mexico, and we'll go camping at this site a Navajo friend of mine owns. We'll be back here in no time."

130

"Ah, yeah...good plan, but I'm leaving. My ticket is already booked. I can't miss my flight." She had known I was going back, so I didn't know why she was teasing me with a great adventure I could never go on.

"Simple, Cheryl. Just change your flight!" She might have added the word "duh," because that was certainly the tone of her voice.

Sure enough, the Universe was colluding with Allison's plan. There was only a ten-dollar fee to change my flight, and Jim was fine with our adventure plan too, except for the fact that he wanted to come with us. Allison explained that she couldn't bring a crew of white people up to Hopi. And since we would be sharing a single bed for the night we stayed there, we couldn't possibly bring him Jim. He was disappointed because white people only got to stay in Hopi if they were invited there. Going there was both an honor and a privilege. I felt a little bit bad for him, but we really didn't want any guys hanging out with us. It was girl time!

Our drive up to Hopi was joyful. We sang and laughed all the way. At one point during the drive, Allison turned down the radio and quickly glanced over at me as she drove.

"Listen. There's something I need to say to you." She was solemn as she spoke.

"Okay." I didn't have a clue what she was about to say.

"Jim has it really bad for you, you know," she informed me.

"He does?"

"Yes, Cheryl, he does. God, what is the matter with you? Are you blind or something? The guy would do absolutely anything for you. I mean *anything*. Did you honestly not notice?"

"Well, I thought maybe something was going on, but really, I don't want a relationship. I just came out of a thirteen-year marriage. I don't want anything to do with *any* man."

"Look, all I'm saying is you should at least give him a chance. I mean, what could it hurt, right? Maybe you're avoiding something that could be really good for you." She sounded so convincing. "He would be really good to you, you know. And hey, if it doesn't work out, then no harm done!"

"I don't know..." I turned my head to look out the car window. I was just not interested in a relationship, especially now that I'd had a taste of being just myself. "I'll think about it."

She knew I was done talking about it and she left it at that. But she did bring it up many more times during the trip, enough that I would eventually break down and follow her advice when I returned back to Sedona. For now, I just wanted to do our road trip.

Hopi was situated smack in the middle of the Navajo Nation. Although the landscape was beautiful and at times even breathtaking, driving through the Nation was very hard on my heart. Poverty abounded. Dilapidated shacks used as homes were strewn throughout the land. At every rundown gas station we passed, small packs of abandoned and diseased dogs ran wild. Trash and discarded items were scattered along the roadside everywhere. My heart went out to these people. I sent out prayers asking for forgiveness for what my ancestors had done. I offered a private wish of love, hoping for peace in return. I knew on some level, somewhere, my prayers would be received.

Hopi sat atop a large mesa in the middle of nowhere. As we followed the exit off the nearly deserted highway, Allison began to lay down the rules. No taking pictures, no asking about ceremonies, don't venture past the property line without a Hopi member with you, always keep your legs covered to the knee, and on and on it went. I understood why she was drilling me so hard, but it became rather hard to take. I had become fairly good with people by now, and I wasn't a complete idiot. I don't know if she was nervous for me or for herself because she was responsible for me while on their land.

We pulled up to an old trailer home. Just as elsewhere in the Navajo Nation, dogs ran rampant. Although they looked the same, these dogs had owners who fed them. Before we stepped through the open door of the mobile home, I was surprised by one of the largest screen TVs I had ever seen. What a shock it was; judging from the exterior of the place, you couldn't guess they even owned a TV.

Donald was the head of the household. He lived here with his son Robert. Everyone was so friendly that I felt at home right away. These were my kind of people. No bullshit, no airs—they were good, honest people with big, beautiful hearts. They helped to subdue the mighty fear of God Allison had instilled in me with all her rules.

I sat on a comfy old sofa talking with the young Hopi boy, Robert. He was an absolute delight. I felt his heart immediately. I had never met anyone like him before. He radiated love like the sun, his eyes danced and laughed, and he wore a permanent smile on his face. He was about the same age as my son Brandon, and I took a motherly type of liking to him immediately.

We sat chatting for an hour, and I described what the land was like back home with the Rocky Mountains and ocean. He wanted every detail I could provide as he had only ever known this desert land. Next, I told him the story of the mother of all spiders, the tarantula, that had come to visit me just a few days before. He actually gasped out loud and put his hand to his mouth, which surprised me. Wouldn't a child of the desert be familiar with such creatures? But I laughed, thinking perhaps he was terrified of spiders too.

He slowly brought his hand away from his mouth and dropped it to his lap. The look on his face grew serious and for the first time since we'd met, he wasn't smiling. What was wrong? Immediately I did a quick mental review of what I might have said that offended him.

Finally, after a long, painful pause, he spoke. "Cheryl! Do you know how special that is?"

"No, I guess not. Why is it special?" I was completely perplexed.

"That was Grandmother Spider who came to visit you. She

was bringing the magic of the Spider Clan to you!" His look of excitement told me I should have understood what he had just said, but I didn't. It sounded like a child's fantasy tale, and I felt like a dumb white person. Noticing my confusion, he continued.

"Here, I'll show you," he said. He tugged at the silver chain around his neck until he could get his fingers around the pendant it held. "Look!"

My eyes immediately dropped to the round silver pendant in his hand. I was taken aback to see a large black spider engraved in it.

"Me and my family, we belong to the Spider Clan!" he continued. "And Grandmother Spider coming to visit you? That is very good, very good!"

The knowledge of Grandmother Spider's visit only helped to strengthen the instant bond between us. We spent the rest of the afternoon out in the back of the property. The young Hopi boy was excited to share his knowledge of every plant and rock in the area. Not only did he teach me many plant names, but he also shared the knowledge of the medicine they carried and how to use it.

Later that evening, we sat out in lawn chairs with Donald, talking and watching the sky. It seemed like all we did was laugh and it felt good. Donald and I shared the same sense of humor, most of which was at Allison's expense. To most indigenous people, teasing is a way of showing love and acceptance. And I loved to show my love!

I could feel our playtime coming to a close. Donald finished his soda and looked over at the two of us, knowing we were getting ready to call it a night.

"Well," he said, looking out into the distance, "don't know what I'm going to do after this. Guess I'm gonna have to find me some trouble once you two go in."

I looked at him, still revved up from our night of joking. Without even thinking, the words came out of my mouth.

"Well, you could just go find yourself a woman and bring her back here in your truck, park in front of the open door of your house, and tell her you're taking her to the drive-in movies, 'cause that is one big-ass TV! I mean, geez, Donald, you've got your own personal drive-in theater here! You need to take advantage of it—it could help you get more chicks!"

Donald and Allison turned their heads to look at me at the same time. Donald's face was blank and Allison let out a gasp and covered her mouth with her hand. There was a moment of pure silence, and I thought for sure I had just gotten myself banned from the reservation forever.

Suddenly, Donald burst out in a loud belly laugh. He swung his hand down to hit his thigh and flung his legs up in the air. That nearly sent him toppling backward in his flimsy lawn chair, making him laugh even harder. Allison burst out laughing too. Their laughter was contagious, and soon the three of us were all laughing so hard we had tears in our eyes.

As we readied ourselves for bed that night, Allison made sure I knew what an honor had been bestowed on me by young Robert. She made it clear that the Hopi people don't share knowledge with just any white person who visits. I would need to be sure to offer my gratitude one more time in the morning.

That night I had the worst sleep of my life. I tossed and turned incessantly, and each time I was pulled awake from my overpowering dreams about DNA. While the dreams were strong, they weren't really coherent, and I couldn't make sense of them at all.

In the morning, Allison hopped out of bed, eager to get started with the day.

"How'd you sleep?" she asked, bubbling with good cheer.

"Really shitty, actually." I rubbed my forehead. I felt almost as if I was hungover. "I kept waking up all night long—it was horrible. Over and over I had dreams of DNA going through my head. It was like it was being forced into my brain, because now my head hurts."

She sat down next to me on the bed and talked in a whisper so the others, who were now in the kitchen starting breakfast, wouldn't hear.

"Cheryl, they say the Hopi carry the original DNA of man... they were the seed people brought here from the world before this." Her voice was hushed.

"Brought here by who?" I whispered back.

She pointed up to the sky and then I understood. I knew exactly who she meant: the Star People. Because I already had a connection to these beings, I now understood why I was intuitively picking up on this in my dreams. I was happy to know my intuition was starting to work a little again. And perhaps my connection to those guys "up there" had a greater effect on me than I was aware of.

The next two days were filled with adventure and travel. Robert ended up coming camping with us and then stayed the night with Allison after she dropped me off back in Sedona. After our excursion, Robert was anxious to get back home onto his land.

While we were camping on the Navajo land, we'd had an extremely sleepless night and an amazing experience with what Robert believed to be Skin-Walkers. Both Hopi and Navajo legends talk about these darker forces. They are believed to be actual people who have the ability to shape-shift into any animal they choose, as long as they wear the skin of that animal on their body. Skin-Walkers are like witches who call on the darker forces for their power, and their intentions are always evil.

In the morning, after our night of terror, we stepped outside of our tiny rented camper trailer to find we were surrounded by friendly, wild dogs. Some were right on our steps, others were lying down. Everywhere we looked, there was a dog. That was the final indication to Robert that Skin-Walkers had indeed been here. We learned that dogs are their natural enemy, and they will instinctively try to protect people when they sense the presence of these evil witches.

I can't say I would have believed the legend before, but after that night, I began to think there was some truth to it. All Robert wanted to do was return to his own land where he was safe and where the medicine of his people prevented passage of a Skin-Walker onto their land.

After we arrived back at Jim's, Allison and I gave Robert a tour of the well-landscaped property. It was dusk and the sun was nearly gone. There was just enough light left for us to see what was directly in front of us. The three of us stood near the manmade pond that was surrounded by smooth, round river rocks. I walked toward the others, trying carefully not to slip on the rocks, when suddenly out from under a crevice bolted a large, hairy tarantula. It was heading straight for me.

I instinctively began to scream and in a flash, I was running toward the house.

Robert quickly spotted the enormous spider. "Oh no! Wait, Cheryl. Wait, Grandmother, I want to talk to you!" he called. "Stop screaming, Cheryl, and just stop moving. You're scaring Grandmother."

"Ahhh!" My shrill scream rang out. "Screw your grandmother, Robert!" I didn't look back at them as I yelled. All I heard was laughter behind me. I just kept running.

When we met inside, Robert and Allison still couldn't stop laughing. I'm not really sure what was so funny about a person running in terror from a monstrous, killer spider. I had to breathe deeply to calm myself.

"Hey, Robert," I said over his laughter. "You know why your Grandmother was here, don't you?"

He finally got serious for a moment. "No, why?"

"Honey, Grandmother was here to tell you that you *are* protected and you are safe. The medicine of your people is with you...even here."

A look of deep relief washed over him. He knew it was true.

Now, he would be able to sleep soundly, knowing Grandmother Spider had brought the power of his land to him.

For the entire six months I remained in Sedona, I never again saw another tarantula.

·❦· *13* ·❦·

*M*en Say the Darndest Things

Perhaps needless to say, I did end up dating Jim. No fireworks were going off for me, but he was a very nice guy and we got along for the most part. He certainly was not a fan of my smoking habit, and I made sure to never do it in front of him. Since our homes were nearly a four-hour plane ride apart, we decided it would be easier if I stayed with him in Sedona. I still kept my hippie house, because I didn't know how long term my new arrangements would be. All of my work was now web design and, with the Internet, I could do that from anywhere in the world. The cards were still selling in North America, but they were no longer on the best-seller's list in Canada. I put very little energy into them now and that was evident in their sales. If it wasn't for the website work, I would have starved.

Although the relationship wasn't food for my soul, Sedona was. Being out in the warmth and sunshine day after day nurtured me. Putting my feet into the red earth and hiking to the caves grounded my energy and made my spirit sing. I absolutely loved Sedona. I made sure to be outside as much as possible.

It was early evening and dusk was just passing. It was the

beginning of the rainy season, and the sky was filled with ominous billowing black clouds. I took advantage of the break from the rain and went out by the hot tub to have a cigarette. I was just about finished when a strange, warbling, humming sound started to grow from the distance, coming from the southern sky. The closer it came, the louder it became. It was as if it had come straight from a movie soundtrack—an erratic humming that grew louder then quieter on each pulse.

I didn't know what the heck it was and I could see nothing in the sky. By the time it was overhead I was crouching down because it felt close enough to hit me. It didn't though. The erratic humming pulse passed me and headed toward the north.

I quickly stubbed out my cigarette and went running for the house. As soon as I had the door open, I was hollering and hunting for Jim. I had just made it to the living room when he stepped out of the washroom. As soon as I saw him I began to ramble about the strange sound from the sky.

We moved to the window and I pointed to the blackness to the north, where the sound had traveled. Within a minute, the entire sky suddenly lit up in a flash. It was so bright that it was like daylight for a few seconds, and we could see every detail of landscape as if it were mid-afternoon. But this time there was no sound at all—just a silent light show.

Both of us jumped back from the window at the same time. We turned to look at each other with wide eyes and open mouths.

"What the hell was that?" Jim said.

"I don't know, but it certainly wasn't lightning!" My heart was beating heavily.

"No, that wasn't lightning. It was like something exploded!" I just stood there nodding my head in agreement.

Just a few moments later, the phone rang. It was Jim's partner, who lived on the north side of town. He had called to ask if we had heard the explosion. Although we had seen it, we hadn't heard anything. It must have been too far away by then. Jim hung up the phone. He was both excited and frightened as he relayed his version of the conversation he'd just had with his partner.

"He was in his office and his wife was in the living room when suddenly one of the largest explosions he had ever felt went off. It shook the house and windows, like an earthquake. Apparently, it shook the whole neighborhood, because they went running outside to see what it was and nearly every person in the subdivision was already out there. I told him what you had heard outside, just moments before, and he thinks maybe it was some kind of craft that crashed." After the long-winded story, Jim needed a breath.

"Really? Well, I would have to agree, because I've never heard a warbling sound like that before. So what are you doing? Let's go!" I turned to head toward the door.

"Whoa, whoa, Cheryl. Hold on...go where?"

"Let's go find the crash! Come on!"

"Cheryl, we can't go look for that crash," he said reasonably. "For two reasons. First, wherever it's crashed, up there in the north, there are no roads, and we can't go out on foot because it would take us all night. Second, you can bet government intelligence is already on their way. You don't want to have them find *you* at an alien crash site."

I stared at him with a look that said I thought he was nuts for not wanting to go. Since I didn't have my own car here, I was at his mercy. If I did have a vehicle, all he would have been looking at now was a trail of dust.

For the next couple of days we read all the little local newspapers, but there was no mention of the powerful explosion that rocked the northern residents of Sedona. We could have been jumping to conclusions, but to Jim and I it smelled like a government cover-up.

A couple of days later the two of us were on a plane heading back to my place. Although I loved it here in Sedona, it was vital to me that I saw Jaden on a regular basis. For the first time, my girlfriends would be meeting my boyfriend, which was a very strange feeling for me. It was like showing off a new car. My being in a relationship was a shock to everybody. No one was going to be more surprised than Brent, and I cringed at the thought of having to tell him the real reason I had been in Sedona all this time.

It was mid-afternoon when the phone rang. Jim and I had just arrived the day before. When I saw Brent's number on the call display, I immediately headed for my bedroom. I really wanted to do this in private.

"How's it going?" I asked in the most casual voice I could muster. I wasn't sure if I was hiding my nervousness though.

"It's good, Cheryl. Things are all good," Brent replied. "I'd like to talk to you if you have a minute."

I felt a wave of relief I wasn't going to be the one starting a heavy conversation. I thought this would give me the opening I needed. "For sure I have time. What's up?"

"Well," he said, hesitating. His voice was a bit shaky and I could tell he was nervous. "I've done a lot of thinking lately, Cheryl. I just really wanted to call and apologize to you."

I felt a hot flash of emotion rush up my throat. I listened quietly as he continued. "I see now how much I hurt you by not being there for you. I see how much I shut you out and tried to shut you down too. I'm sorry I didn't really listen to you when you needed to be heard. I see now that all you wanted to do was try to work out our problems, and I'm sorry I blamed you for being the problem."

He paused for a breath, then continued on. "I thought if you went and fixed yourself, then there would be no problems. I was clueless. I see now I was the problem. You are walking your path and growing and I have been stuck all these years. I really honestly love you, Cheryl. I see now just how wrong I was and how much I must have hurt you...and I'm sorry."

Tears were trickling down my face. This man, whom I still very much loved, was now trying to make amends with me. I had waited years for him to open his eyes and himself to me, as he used to when we first met. Why now? Of all the times in our lives, why now? My heart was breaking again. He was my soul mate, the love of my life, and it pained me so much. I had only just started to get on with my life.

As much as I had wanted this, I felt he still wasn't ready. If he didn't plunge passionately into his own personal growth and spiritual life, I just couldn't do it with him again. I was going to have to keep on living my life until then. I couldn't stand around holding my breath for him. I had already spent years doing that.

I thanked him deeply, then as gently as I could, I delivered the news I was now with someone else. I'm not sure who hurt more from that, me or him. We talked and cried for almost two hours on the phone. He was heartbroken and completely devastated.

When we finally hung up, I put a cold facecloth to my red and swollen face. As I looked in the mirror at myself, I silently spoke what I felt deep in my heart. *If you are ever ready, Brent, I will come back—I'll wait for you. If we are never to be together again, then I wish you all the best the world has to offer. Just know I will love you, always and forever. No man will ever replace you.*

Now that everything was clear and out in the open, I felt a huge sense of relief and freedom. After spending some quality time with my little guy, I headed back to Sedona with Jim. The bright sun and wonderful energy of the land was exactly what I needed.

Within a few days of my return to Sedona, I received a call from Allison. She had been having private discussions with Juan, the Mayan priest, on the phone for the last two weeks. He had invited her to visit his home in South America for a couple of weeks. He felt it would be easier to communicate in person.

"I want you to come with me," Allison said.

She had caught me off guard and it took me a moment to assess it. "You do? But why? I mean...you don't need me. I know you're going so you can take care of your business with him, but..."

I felt that old familiar sensation pulling at my heart. "All right, I'll go. When do you want to leave?"

"I'd like to be out of here in a week. I'll drive to Sedona and grab you, then we'll head to the Phoenix airport from there, okay?"

"Sounds sweet, Allison." By the time I got off the phone, I was thoroughly energized. I had never been to any place like South America! I did a little happy dance, then headed off to find Jim to tell him the great news.

He was downstairs working on his computer when I came busting in to tell him my good news. But his reaction was the opposite of what I expected. "You're *what?*" He sounded incredulous, obviously not sharing my excitement.

"I'm going to South America," I repeated slowly, because apparently he hadn't gotten it the first time.

"How in the hell could you make a decision like that without asking me first?"

If there was a moment when the ear-wrenching scratch of a needle sliding across an old LP record could have sounded, this would be it. It happened inside my head and my happy dance came to a halt. *He didn't just say what I thought he just said, did he? Did he say "ask"? Did he really say "ask"?* I probably would have accepted the word *talk*, but I simply could not accept the word *ask*. I shouldn't need permission from anyone. I stood there staring at him as that old familiar boil started pumping through my veins. He mistakenly took that as a sign he should continue.

"You think it's okay to just traipse off with your friends without discussing it with me first? You're not going down there. There's guerillas and crime everywhere. Two women alone? It's not safe! You know what? You're not going down there. I forbid it!"

Oh my, this guy just didn't know when to stop. Unfortunately for him, he was going to get a taste of my full fury for the first time. My heart started to pound as the effects of the adrenaline rushed through my body. I could not believe he had actually said the word *forbid. Forbid?* Just who in the hell did he think he was, anyway? *Nobody forbids me to do anything! I am my own boss and no man will ever make a decision for me or tell me what to do!*

I completely lost it on him. He didn't have a chance. This was war and I was going to fight to the death if I had to. My freedom was at stake! I cursed him out like I was a nasty, dirty-talking little thug! All signs of the healed version of me had vanished, and all that remained was the old reactive, hot-tempered, street-fighting kid from years ago.

I don't think he knew what hit him either, but by the time I was done he wouldn't talk to me. To be honest, I didn't even care. I stormed off to be alone. He could just sit there and rot right now, as far as I was concerned. I didn't give a shit what he did.

I headed outside, slamming the door behind me. I walked up the trail and over to the hot tub area. The stillness of the evening and the clear, starry sky slowly brought peace back to my rage-filled mind. The warm air wrapped around me like a blanket of comfort, which put my angry sobs to rest. I sat on a large rock that was still warm from a day in the squelching sun. After half an hour or so, normal Cheryl was back and the Incredible Hulk version of me had dissipated back into the darkness.

Now that I was thinking clearly, I looked at the reaction I'd just had and why I had been triggered so badly. I couldn't allow myself to get away with that kind of behavior. I mean, certainly I was angry, but I had just totally lost my mind. So what was the trigger? Of course it was the authority—I always reacted strongly to anyone who attempted to wield authority over me. But when I looked at it deeply enough, I saw it as an oppression of my personal freedom and power. The real trigger behind it was me—I had oppressed myself all my life. I could only let myself be free to a small degree, and I certainly could never allow myself to have too much power. Jim had become the mirror, reflecting back to me my own deep sense of powerlessness and my inner oppressor.

I knew what I needed to do. I got up, brushed my bottom clean of red dust from the rock, and headed back into the house. I found Jim stretched out on the bed in the spare room downstairs, his hand on his forehead. I felt bad when I looked at him.

"Can I talk to you?" I asked in a tone that told him I had gathered my wits about me.

"Are you going to kill me?" he asked, half joking, but half not.

"No, I've got it together now, Jim. I'm sorry, really. I'd like a chance to explain myself, okay?" I went on to share with him as honestly as I could what the situation had reflected back to me. I made sure I referenced everything at myself, so I owned it, and avoided using the accusatory word "you." I knew how to properly clear my stuff with someone else; I had learned that years ago in the spiritual community with P.T. Mistlberger. I just had to use it. It worked beautifully to open the line of communication between us, and Jim shared his side of things.

"I'm sorry too. I used the wrong choice of words. I was just angry and hurt. You get to go off and have adventures and I am not included in any of them. But you know, Cheryl, it *is* dangerous down there, especially for two women on their own. I just thought if I demanded that you stay, you'd take my concerns seriously. I'm sorry."

"All right, I understand, Jim. I do. You just have to know something, though. I cannot be kept. I cannot be caged and captured like a bird. In my heart I need to fly, to be free. I can't help that. Now, if you're not sure you can live with that, then we shouldn't be in a relationship." I was clear and firm, but kind.

"Of course I can live with that. I wouldn't want anything less. But I also need to be included in your life. You have to allow me to be a part of it. You also need to at least respect my opinion even if you don't agree with it."

I completely agreed. I had pretty much held him at arm's length in my life up till now. He was a really good man and person.

He never again made a statement about not allowing me to do something. It was an off moment for him and for me, but it was a beautiful opportunity for growth and personal insight. For that, I had gratitude.

⋘ *14* ⋙

When in Doubt, Get Bossy

Before long I headed off with Allison to visit Juan. Jim still had concerns for our safety, but I assured him we would never go anywhere without Juan or a member of his family with us. It was a good plan, but it didn't help when I had to make my way through International Arrivals at the airport.

After a ridiculously long travel time, both Allison and I were exhausted when we finally got off the plane. Fortunately, she knew just enough Spanish to help us get through customs. Once through, we had to claim our luggage. We both grabbed our bags and exited the airport, but the procedure was much different than I had experienced before. As we came around a corner, we were not greeted by a mass of people all waiting for their loved ones. They were all outside; no one was allowed to wait inside. Instead, we were met by three or four members of the military. Unlike in North America, these soldiers carried the largest type of automatic guns I had ever seen in real life. I was utterly terrified when I saw them.

They were directing people through another single-file security check. Each passenger had to stand still while dogs sniffed at their clothes and luggage. Then each piece of luggage was put onto a rotating belt for a final x-ray check. I thought it strange, as we had gone through security before boarding, but I guess they can't be too careful when it comes to drug trafficking. I was scared to death and to make matters worse, Allison had been shuffled about twenty people back from me.

I was just getting ready to take my bag off the x-ray belt when a soldier approached me and grabbed my shirt by the sleeve. I let out a yelp like a little dog would have. He began speaking Spanish in a loud, fast-paced voice. Uncomprehending, I looked at him with fearful eyes.

The only thing I could get out was, *"Yo no hablo español,"* which means, "I don't speak Spanish." That was the only sentence I knew.

He continued to talk at me in his native language as he pulled me away. With me in one hand and my luggage in his other hand, he was hauling us both off to somewhere unknown. My legs were shaking violently, and I kept looking back to find Allison, while I vainly tried to tell him I had a friend back there.

What was happening? I thought they might have found something in my luggage. What if someone had used me as a drug mule and I didn't know it? Was I going to be taken off to some nightmare of a prison where I would rot away for years and no one could help me? What if this guy was actually a bad guy playing for the other team and had decided I would make good ransom bait? I thought I might literally pee in my pants, the terror was that strong.

I was surprised and astounded when he dragged both me and my bags out a set of doors that led to a waiting crowd of people. He surveyed the mob, but in no way relinquished his fast grip on my shirt. I frantically scoured the crowd for the only face I knew. Finally, I saw him approaching us from the back of the crowd. I yelled his name, fearing he might somehow overlook me and the soldier with the machine gun, who had become my new accessory.

As soon as Juan was close enough, he began talking to the guard. I had no idea what they said to each other, but after a couple of minutes the soldier let me go. It appeared my luggage and I had been officially claimed. Once I was free, I flung my arms around Juan's neck with a death grip of gratitude and relief. I didn't want to let go! He hugged me back at first, then patted my back as a sign to let go.

I slid myself off of him and looked up into his eyes. They were the same kind and smiling eyes I remembered. He was grinning ear to ear.

"*Hola, hola*, Cheryl. How are you? Good flight, yes?" I could hardly hear him over the noisy crowd.

At that moment Allison made her way out of the door and we all hugged in a quick and happy reunion. But the noise and confusion and getting jostled around was causing me to feel disoriented, and all I wanted to do was get the hell out of there. Once we had made our way to the parked car, Allison started in right away.

"What on earth was going on in there, Cheryl? One minute I'm standing in line and the next thing I know, I look up to see you getting hauled away!" She was apparently as surprised as I was at what had happened.

Once Juan and his son had our bags in his SUV, I put my hand on his arm and began to speak slowly. "Juan, why did the guard hold me? What did he say to you?" I asked.

Juan tilted his head slightly and then gave me a big smile. "Oh, it was good—everything is good. The guard, he hold you, he make sure no one steal you, *si?*" And he started to chuckle. "Everything is very, very, good," he managed to say through his thick accent and limited English.

I sneaked a sidelong look at Allison and gave her a look that said *Oh my God*, and she returned a secret look of shock. Even she hadn't expected it to be like this. She threw her arm around me and touched her forehead to mine.

"Let's get outta here!" she said. I happily jumped into the back seat with my friend, looking forward to the drive down the mountain through the lush green jungle.

Evening fell upon us shortly after we started our descent down the mountainside into the city, where Juan lived so his children could attend school. I was very disappointed—I had been so looking forward to being among the trees and wild jungle for the first time. Juan said that he truly wished to live in seclusion and from the land, but for now he would sacrifice his own needs for his kids'. It wouldn't be until morning that I would get a full understanding of what it was like in this city he called home.

Allison and I were staying with Juan and his wife, along with his children, who ranged in age from three to thirty years old. He lived in a small, humble apartment that rose high above the city. In the morning, I headed outside with a strong cup of coffee to have a cigarette. It was warm and muggy and the sun was barely breaking through the clouds. I decided to sit away from the main doors, near a tiny pool and outdoor restroom. As I gazed around, I felt for a moment that I had been put into a compound or a women's penitentiary. A solid brick wall of at least ten feet in height completely encircled the building. On top of it was strung razor-sharp barbed wire that had been twisted into circles. It spiraled menacingly along the entire length of the wall. At the entrance stood a guard shack that monitored the gateway into the building. Two guards stayed inside the shack, while a third patrolled the grounds. There seemed only one difference between this and a federal jail: everything here was in place to keep the bad guys outside, not inside.

For the first eight days I remained mostly quiet. Juan's wife was more fluent in English and we got along very well. But other than joking around and playing during the free time, I did not speak when Allison and Juan started up. Gradually, they had been coming head to head. Each day their discussions grew increasingly heated. I know this might sound ironic because of my past and my outbursts, but I've always been uncomfortable with people fighting. I only ever want peace. I become shaky and upset when I am around anyone who is angry or arguing. After days and days of confrontation and tempers slowly escalating, I felt it necessary to step in. It seemed that this was the first time Juan really noticed me.

I offered insight into their differences and helped the two come to a place where they could present their ideas and thoughts without the heat of arguing. At that point I became a participating member in their discussions, but I still spoke only when necessary. This helped to strengthen the bond between me, Juan, and his family. Poor Allison was having such a hard go of it all. It hurt her to see their acceptance of me—at her expense, it seemed—and I felt bad, so I did what I could to help put things back together for her.

One day, the three of us sat together to share our encounters with the Star People, as Juan liked to call them. It was a great day. Everyone was getting along and in a great mood. Allison shared her story first, then me, with Juan sharing last. My story was the least dramatic of the tales, but it wasn't until Juan spoke that I knew it was still very relevant. Without relating all of his many personal encounters, Juan explained how the Star People had spoken to him in his head. That drew my attention. But when he described the ship he had been taken aboard, time after time I got shivers down my arms and spine. He described exactly the same craft I had seen outside my window a couple of summers ago. The entire time Juan relayed his description, he looked me straight in the eye. His smile relayed another message to me: we both now knew we shared a common bond. He filled me with reassurance through his eyes. Our discussion ended in a big group hug and I loved that.

We left the confines of the building only a few times. I thought I would suffocate on the powerful diesel fumes that saturated the air in the streets. The driving habits of its citizens were also unlike anything I had witnessed before. Each time I rode in a vehicle, I wasn't sure what would kill me first, carbon monoxide poisoning or the terrifyingly aggressive drivers who tried to take us out on every turn.

In hopes of entertaining his female guests, Juan took me, Allison, and his wife to the mall, which I thought would be uneventful. I was wrong. The entrance to the underground parking housed a guard shack, gate, and multiple guards. Before being allowed to enter, the car was visually inspected on top and beneath, using a mirror attached to a long handle. I looked at Allison with wide eyes.

"Wow, I feel so much better now, knowing there are no car bombs at the mall! It's the safest place in the city for sure!" I joked.

Juan's wife turned to us, not understanding my sarcasm and replied, "See! I told you! We take you only to safe places."

"Oh yes, safe, safe, safe!" Allison said as she laughed. That got me going too, but mine was nervous laughter.

Inside the mall were more ominous safeguards. Every security guard wore a dark, military-style uniform and a huge gun across the front of his chest. It was as if we were caught inside a bad action film. It would be easy to confuse the mall security for a bad guy's goons. I caught my breath at my first glance of the guards. Seeing their guns sent a wave of nausea sweeping through my stomach. I wasn't really keen on going shopping amid all those weapons!

We now had five days left before my departure back to North America. The plan had been that Allison would stay for an additional week or two after me, as she needed the time with Juan. I had brought my laptop with me and was able to work a little here and there. Up to that point, I still hadn't shared a word about my work with the fractals, the cards, or anything related to intuitive work. I don't often talk about myself and am extremely humble about my work. It was only at Allison's prodding that I opened up at all.

I brought out a fresh deck of cards and made a gift of them to Juan's wife. She was in love with them right away. She and Juan sat on their bed doing readings for themselves while admiring every image in the deck. I explained what fractals were and the mathematics behind them. Juan was fascinated. Their interest and response to the cards encouraged me to show them something more, something I had shared with only a small number of people.

Years ago, I created a video movie. While I was meditating one day, the entire layout for the short video was downloaded into my brain. I didn't really like that description, but I didn't know any other way to explain it. I understood how it was to flow, what images to include, and most clearly, the message it was to contain. Then, just as in the movie of *Close Encounters of the Third Kind*, I became obsessed with creating it. I worked every day, late into the evening. I couldn't stop until it was complete. Back then the programs used to create your own movie from scratch were complicated. So I had to learn how to use the program before I could make the movie. Regardless of the small delay, the film was complete in less than a week. I named it *The Greatest Mystery*. I played it at only a few talks at home and a few times in Sweden. Other than that, it remained hidden away on my computer.

I had the idea to share it with my new friends, who now felt like my family. As we did every other night, we all gathered on Juan's large bed. It was the gathering place for hanging out and chatting. Juan, his wife, his oldest and youngest sons, and Allison and I all huddled together on the bed. With the laptop ready, we dimmed the lights and the show began.

Juan's wife translated the words from the video as image after image flowed. Fractals of Guides and Spirit Beings filled the screen, while their message to humanity was shared. Powerful, trancelike music filled the room. My audience was captivated. No one made a sound except for the quiet translation in the background. When it was done, the younger son jumped up and returned the room to light. I turned to look at Juan and his wife with a smile on my face. I was going to ask if they liked it, but remained silent when I saw them. The two of them had tears flowing down their faces, and

Juan had his hand over his heart. It took him a minute to gather his thoughts before he began to speak.

In his rough English, he tried to convey what he felt inside. "Cheryl, this is very, very beautiful. This message does not come from you, no? This come from Spirit, I know this. Many times when they take me, they tell me this message. Your message is that message, the message for all of humanity. This I know. I love you, my sister Cheryl. You have touched my heart and I thank you for sharing this with us." His tears glistened on his dark skin. His hand still remained on his heart. With his free hand, he reached out to me and we embraced in a long hug.

Now I was crying—we were all crying! For the first time since my arrival, I had allowed myself to really take up space. I allowed my work to be seen and heard. I then shared with him the story of how the video came to be. Juan completely understood when I said my Guides had put it into my head. He just listened and smiled and nodded his head.

What I shared with him next, I had told no one else but Brent. A few years earlier, when I questioned my teachers about who was helping me to make the fractals, I was given a reply: "An Indian will give you a clue."

To some, the phrase might seem derogatory, but it was only at this very moment that I understood why they had used it back then.

Sitting before me was a Mayan priest who had traveled throughout South and North America, learning the ways of all the indigenous tribes. He called himself an Indian and he said it with pride. He used the word as a way to describe the many cultures and traditions that had sculpted him into the man he was today.

I was so moved and extremely grateful that the little prophecy I had received so many years ago while on my bedroom floor had come to fruition. Although I knew what Juan had told me was true, I still told no one when asked where I received my guidance from. It was the message itself, not where it came from, that was important.

We all shared many hugs, laughs, and good times before I returned home. I was almost unbearably sad to leave. I loved my new family and they loved me. We vowed we would remain in touch and see one another again.

Despite my sorrow at leaving, it was nice to return to the seclusion Sedona offered after being in an apartment filled with so many people. Jim worked most days and I was left to my own devices. I preferred it that way. The more alone time I had, the happier I was.

Shortly after my return, we headed off on a road trip to Los Angeles. Jim had to attend an opening for a film he was involved with. We bickered quite a bit on that trip, as neither of us was used to the aggressive driving or strange energy of this overpopulated city. Every time I walked for any distance, I was overcome with the oddest sensation that I had suddenly fallen knee-deep into the ground. It happened often enough that I nearly ended up on my face a few times. I wasn't able to figure out what that was all about. The only memorable thing to come out of that trip was an extravagant lunch date with some of the cast members of the movie, which included Dr. Masaro Emoto. He was a lovely man with an incredible sense of humor. I sat next to his business partner Hans from Austria. A charming man, he became my smoking buddy back at the hotel for the rest of our stay.

I was beginning to tire of all the traveling at this point. If I wasn't on a plane, then I was in a car going somewhere. I was looking forward to having a few weeks of rest and peace before we headed home to British Columbia, where I had organized several talks for Juan.

During one of the quiet evenings at home in Sedona, Jim had invited his good friend Tom Dongo to drop by. Tom was one of the premier UFO and paranormal researchers in the country. Not only was he the go-to guy for many government agencies, but he had also been featured numerous times on film and TV. He had written several fascinating books on his area of expertise and offered UFO sky-watching tours in Sedona. Tom had a massive personal photo album containing original photographs of UFOs, spirits, and some of the most strange and enthralling paranormal phenomena I had ever seen. The photo diary spanned decades of cases and studies Tom had worked on. One by one, he told the story behind each photo.

My desire was now ignited to visit the old ranch where many of Tom's pictures had been taken. The next day Jim and I headed out in his pickup truck to visit the place, which had now been seized by the government.

The old dirt road had been washed out from year after year of seasonal heavy rains. We had to drive at a turtle's pace because of the huge divots and potholes in the abandoned road. I could have gotten out and walked faster than the truck moved. We were used to this, though, as we came up here nearly once a week to hunt for UFOs in the sky. Today, we were heading down the other side of the small mesa into the valley below, to the ranch itself.

It was mid-afternoon and hot. Once we descended into the valley it was even hotter. The ranch's entire property was fenced, and every few feet large official government signs warned visitors of the penalties of trespassing on this property. Neither Jim nor I was willing to test the threat, so we walked the perimeter and kept a safe distance. Down here, the feeling of being watched was much more intense than I had ever experienced at the top of the mesa. It was creepy.

When it was time to leave, Jim decided to drive around a small loop in the driveway so he didn't have to back up. He soon regretted the choice, because just as we started around it, we landed in deep, loose sand. He attempted to back up and got us half turned around when the two back tires sunk into the sand trap.

Jim was instantly upset. He knew full well the consequences of being stuck in a desert in the middle of nowhere. We both hopped out of the truck to assess the situation. As soon as I had my door open, I felt a hundred eyes watching me. The feeling of being observed was even worse here than over at the ranch. Worse still, they felt much closer, as though they were swarming around the truck. My stomach dropped when I saw the back bumper was only a couple of inches off the ground. Jim started to curse, which he didn't do often. We had only a half-empty bottle of water each and there was no cell-phone reception down here. We were stuck and alone. It would take hours to get to a paved road from here, let alone to a populated area.

Though we were nervous and frightened, we did our best to get ourselves out of the sand. I'd try giving the truck gas while Jim pushed from the rear. Then he would come and take the wheel, trying to rock forward and back again, but it was all in vain. The engine would scream and wail with every push on the gas pedal. It was no use, though. We were going nowhere fast and sinking the truck deeper down with each try. The air was thick with dust now, making it hard to breathe. The dirt in my mouth only made my thirst more intense, but I couldn't drink what little water I had. The two of us were tired and filthy with dust-covered sweat, and I could tell from Jim's behavior that we were in serious trouble.

He hopped back in the truck to give it another try. We had already been out here for over forty minutes now and it didn't look like freedom was on the way either. This was the last shot. If we couldn't get the truck out, we would have to start walking. I stood at the back trying to push while Jim rocked the truck back and forth with the accelerator. That's when I knew this was it—we needed help beyond what I could provide. I began to bellow a mental command to those who I knew were watching us.

All right, listen up! I am sending out a distress call. You guys are here in my dimension, in my reality, and by Universal law you must help me. I damn well know you're here. You need to get this truck out of the sand now!

I no sooner had gotten the last word out when the truck jumped out of the holes and rolled onto solid ground. I started screaming and jumping, yelling my thanks. I ran over to Jim's window, still jumping and hollering, "They did it! They did it!"

He stepped out of the truck and I started talking at him, all excited. I told him what I had mentally yelled at the invisible watchers. He looked down at the deep holes in the sand and said, "Well, I don't know how else we would have gotten out of this. Look at the bumper mark in the sand—we actually dug ourselves down that deep. Someone pushed us out and it wasn't you!" He said, looking down at me. I was no bigger than an average twelve-year-old child. It certainly wasn't me who pushed us out. "Whatever it was," Jim continued, "I'm thankful!"

It's one of those stories a person could easily roll their eyes at and think, "Yeah, right! Like that really happened." But that is really how it happened. Whether it was coincidence or not, I'm just glad we made it out. We never tempted fate by going down into the valley a second time. In a month or so we would return to the top of the mesa one more time, but not until after we returned from the little talking tour I had set up for Juan back home.

November in Canada is cold. Even though the temperatures are more moderate on the coasts, the frigid torrential rains of the west coast penetrate the skin, freezing you from the inside out. Unused to the low temperatures, poor Juan and his wife nearly froze to death, regardless of how many layers of clothes they wore. With the help of my friends I had managed to set up a couple of talks for Juan, both on the mainland and on Vancouver Island, which was an hour and a half ferry ride away. Of course, I had done this all for free, expecting nothing in return. I just wanted to help my friend.

I caught quite a bit of flack over those talks. Many people were disappointed in the simplicity of the message the Mayan priest had to share. Most were looking for the glamour of the well-known Pleiadian relationship with the Mayan people and the doom and gloom of the end times in 2012. Juan did address those topics, but his message was pure and simple. He spoke of having fire in the heart, as he put it. He told them the most important thing was the heart, not the head. He shared that there was no mother ship coming from outer space to save the people of Earth and we would have to do our own work by becoming heart oriented and connecting to the energies of Mother Earth.

I felt sad for both Juan and all the people who were disappointed. I didn't tell Juan. Why would I? He already had a sour aftertaste over his previous experiences with white people. Our last talk was on the island. By the time it was done, we were all tired and looking forward to a small break. The entire ferry trip back, I was plagued with a feeling of loneliness. I was missing my Guides. I had not heard their voices for over two years now. As we departed the ferry, I began to question Juan on the subject.

"Juan, do you ever feel like you miss the Beings?" I asked.

"No, no," he replied. "For me, I know they are always there. I keep my mind here, on the work I have to do. For me it is not a big deal if they are here or if they are not. I need to focus on the work for my people, not on that." Then he turned to look at me. "You miss them, yes?"

"Yes, I do. Sometimes I feel very alone now because I don't hear them or see them anymore." My sadness was evident in my tone.

"*Si, si*, I understand this, Cheryl. But you just need to keep doing your work and keep the fire in your heart, yes? All other things do not matter." Once again he had delivered a simple but strong message. Get out of your head, get into your heart, and just do the work you have come here to do. Everything else will take care of itself.

I knew he was right, but that didn't stop a couple of tears from making an unwanted escape. I couldn't help how I was feeling. Abandoned once again was the only way to describe it. But that feeling didn't last long, and the next day I had a message on my phone from Leslie at the Coastal Academy. She had helped me in setting up the talks. I replayed her message twice, just so I could fully take it in.

"Hi Cheryl, it's Les. Just wanted you to know a friend of mine called me today who works for the airlines. Apparently, one of the pilots reported seeing a large, moving orange ball of light during his flight from the mainland to the island last night. It was right around the time you should have been on the ferry. What do you think of that?"

I was elated. I wasn't sure if I unconsciously tuned into their energy, which brought on my feelings of loneliness and abandonment, or if the feelings had created the need for an appearance. I didn't care either way. I just reveled in the fact that, indeed, they were still around.

After Juan's departure, Jim and I headed back to Sedona. Winter was beginning to set in up here in the mountains, but the cold just wasn't the same. It was a dry, arid cold without so much as a breeze, which made it quite bearable. The fact that it was still bright and sunny every day was a welcome contrast to the constant gloom of Canada's coastal weather.

Jaden was going to be here soon. I had planned to have him visit me here for a change. I knew how much my little guy liked to travel, and I was sure he would fall in love with Sedona as I had. He would be staying for two weeks and returning home Christmas Eve. Since it was a direct flight, he would travel alone as an unaccompanied minor. Well, that was the original plan.

Shortly before Jaden was due to arrive, Jim and I had spent an hour out in the hot tub one evening just gazing at the wondrous Sedona sky. The city had a low-light law which kept street lights to a minimum. With few lights to interfere, the view of the evening sky was unimpeded. You could always count on seeing something strange up there in the stars if you looked long enough.

After an hour of hot-water soaking, my fingers were wrinkled and pruned. It was time to get out. I threw on my heavy white robe, wrapped my head in a towel, and headed back inside while Jim replaced the cover on the tub. I stepped into the master bedroom and was watching myself in the window, which doubled as a mirror at night. As I pulled the twisted towel from my head, a message stronger than anything I had ever received before utterly overcame me. Although it wasn't a voice, the entire message was worded and carried a strong feeling that nested its way into my cells. *Go home to Brent now. Do this as soon as possible or it's going to be too late.*

I was instantly weak in the knees. I reached out behind me to feel for the bed—I had to sit down or I was going to collapse. I was shaky and needed to close my eyes. Go home to Brent now? I had almost given up on our relationship. We talked on the phone once or twice a week when I called to speak with Jaden. I knew he had finally joined a men's spiritual group and had just begun to have a social life. However, I didn't think he was anywhere near ready to be back with me. He was only just beginning to find himself now, and it had been almost a year. My head told me he needed more time, but I could not ignore the message that had come so strongly.

If I was supposed to go home to Brent, then that was exactly what I'd do. If they had told me what I would be returning to, I would never have made that choice. With absolutely no foresight, however, I blindly devised a plan to get back home.

A few days later I asked Jim if he wanted to go up to the ranch and sky-watch. I figured it would be a good place to let him know of my change of plans. As we drove up the old dirt road, bouncing around, I told him I would be returning with Jaden on Christmas Eve, alone. I explained I needed that time alone with my boys, being it was our first Christmas since the divorce. He didn't take the news too well, and I could hardly blame him. No one wants to spend Christmas alone. As I had expected, we began to fight.

We were now parked at the top of the mesa, where the view

was incredible. I loved getting a peek at the glowing red landscape before nighttime stole our view. We had about another twenty minutes or so before the sun would set completely. The bickering had escalated to angry silence, and I sat inside the truck with my arms folded, fuming, as I carried on a long dialog in my head telling him just exactly what I thought of him. I figured Jim was probably doing the same. During our silence, I was taken with a strong sensation of being stared at through my passenger's side window. Within seconds, the image of two large, black eyes and a round bobble head claimed my inner vision. I couldn't believe it. Of all the times in the world, that little sucker had chosen the wrong time to come into my world. Without giving it a second thought, I gave my peeping visitor a mental cursing out. *You know what buddy? You need to get the hell out. You heard me! I'm not playing this game with you, and you have no right to be in my realm. Now get your ass out of here!*

I no sooner had gotten the words out of my head when the truck's antenna, which was also on the passenger's side, let out a large *ping*. It began to swing wildly back in forth in front of us. It scared the living daylights out of Jim. I burst into laughter. I knew the little bugger had just sent me a little *screw you* back. It really humored me.

"What the hell is that?" Jim said. I could hear anger and fear mixed in his voice.

"I think I know. You didn't see anything hit it, right?" I said, still really humored by the whole incident.

"No, I was sitting here staring at it, and the next thing I know it's swinging back and forth." He took a sharp breath. "It's not like a bat or a bird hit it. I would have seen that, and I don't know of anything else big enough to make it swing like that! Look, it's still going."

Hesitating, I said, "You're not going to believe this, but..." I turned to look at him and explained the story, half laughing about it.

"Cheryl, it isn't funny. You can't just go around cursing them out!" We watched as the pace of the swinging antenna began to slow.

"Ah yes, Jim, I can! I have every right to do whatever I want here. Remember, I'm the one who is incarnated. Therefore, when they visit me like that, into my world, into my reality, they have no power and no rights. They must abide by me. It's really that simple," I said, still smiling.

I knew he did not agree with what I'd said and that he was frightened by the whole thing. Both of us believed the little invisible creature had grabbed the antenna, bent it backward, then let it go, sending it flinging wildly back and forth. I, however, had no fear at all. One day while meditating, just after the craft had made an appearance on the farm, the Guides explained to me how the one who is incarnated has ultimate rule in this third dimension. Anything that does not hold a physical body of some sort does not have power over me here. All I had to do was claim my rights and my power, and without fear, deal with the outsider. I also felt the extra backing of their protection, since it was a part of our agreement that they would keep me safe at all times.

That was to be my final visit to one of my most favorite spots in Sedona. It was a bit awkward between Jim and I over the next few weeks. I told him I would return right after New Year's; however, my real plan was to call him in the new year and tell him I wasn't coming back. I did this only because I didn't want to completely ruin his Christmas. At least this way he could enjoy the holidays with his mother.

Why is it that the Beings give me guidance on what to do without telling me what I am in for? Never would I have remotely guessed what was waiting upon my return to Brent. I didn't know that my entire world would be torn apart or that my faith in the guidance I received would be tested to its limits.

$\backsim\!\!\circ\!\!\sim$ *15* $\backsim\!\!\circ\!\!\sim$

Not Everything Goes as Planned

I was flying back home to try to reconcile with my husband because Spirit had told me to do it. Over the three-hour flight, I had plenty of time to reflect on just how ridiculous that actually sounded. I had no idea where Brent was at as far as getting back together with me. The fact that our flight had been delayed in Phoenix because of a blizzard back home had given me extra time to think, which was usually not a good thing. I was a nervous wreck.

As I laid my forehead against the cool glass of the window, I looked down to the Earth and said goodbye to Arizona one last time. I was really going to miss this place. Jaden was fully settled in, playing his portable game system, and I knew he didn't want me interrupting him. I just stared out the window as my thoughts drifted back to when I had first met Brent.

At the time, I had no desire to be with a man at all. I had recently been released from the hospital because of a suicide attempt, and all I wanted to do was focus on getting myself mentally healthy again. I planned to take a weekend workshop retreat. My girlfriend had warned me it would be tough. I met Brent the night before, because the two sisters he was rooming with were going to be watching Brandon for me. He seemed like a nice guy, but that's all I thought. He wasn't the type I was normally attracted to. I usually went for the arrogant, outspoken, womanizing types. Brent was shy and quiet. Trying to draw him into conversation was almost impossible.

He attended my workshop as an assistant. Each time we had a break, I found myself searching for him. I was strangely, magnetically drawn to him and I didn't have a clue why. I wasn't attracted to him physically. At the time, he was really ill with eczema; his face was swollen and his lips and face had blended together in red abrasions. I couldn't even tell what color his eyes were. I didn't know why I wanted to be around him so much, but I was strangely drawn to him and I couldn't help myself.

During one of the workshop processes, Brent and I had been paired together. I went to sit beside him and placed my hand on his knee. The moment I touched him, I experienced a weird electric shock. It wasn't static, nor was it painful. It was a tingling from the tip of my middle finger running straight up my arm. I had never felt anything like that before.

We ended up becoming good friends for a couple of weeks before moving into a relationship. If we were going to be together, we wanted to do it consciously. For each of us, our own personal and spiritual growth was the top priority. Brent was a tender and patient partner. I had never experienced kindness like that before. I was seen fully, with all my flaws and shortcomings, and yet he loved me. Another great bonus was when his eczema finally started to heal. It was like a present slowly unwrapping itself. I finally got to see his big blue eyes. I knew within a few short weeks I wanted to spend the rest of my life with him.

Brent was also there when I had my first and biggest spiritual happening. We had been together for a couple of months. Along with attending our own separate classes with P.T. Mistlberger each week, we also took the weekend intensive classes when they came up. It was the day after we had completed one of the most powerful workshops yet, early in the morning, and we had just taken Brandon to school. Brent and I sat in the living room, speaking with one of his roommates about a past life experience we all had seemed to share. Nothing of great significance came out of our conversation and everything seemed normal. It wasn't until we had finished and I had gotten up to continue on with our day that I noticed something was different.

It was so powerful and yet so hard to describe, but somehow my perception of reality had altered. I had a feeling of almost being on drugs or in an altered state, because my understanding and normal way of interacting with the world was completely different. My usual crispness of thought had faded. Actually, most of my sense of self had faded. My ability to perceive time had vanished as well. I was overcome with a profound feeling of love. I loved everyone and everything. I had no judgments of anything. All my beliefs about myself and others had disappeared. Anything of a negative nature had slipped from my mind. All simply was as it was. I could see the pure beauty and light of every person around me. I saw their deepest heart, their vulnerability, their purity, their goodness, their innocence, and their love.

It was not just a moment of insight, it was an entire day of being in a highly enlightened state. My ego mind had been moved to the side, and all that remained was my highest self seeing everyone else's highest self. Brent told me the next day, after it had passed, that it was like looking at God and having God look back at him. It was one of the most profound experiences he had ever had as well. Never had he felt that kind of love or light radiate from another human being before.

I don't know why or how it happened or why it ended when I went to sleep that night. It just did. One of the beautiful gifts to come from that experience, however, was that it deepened our commitment to doing personal growth work, for ourselves and with each other.

It hurt now to look back at those memories. I cherished them deeply. I had never really wanted to leave Brent, but I didn't know any other way to get him to wake up again. It seemed to have worked in some way, because he was now back working with P.T. It wasn't to the same degree as when we were in the community with P.T. thirteen years earlier, but once a week at his men's group was certainly a good start.

But the best ideas never go as planned, no matter how "unplanned" they are. I got off that plane with absolutely no plan other than to get back together with Brent. I don't think any amount of planning could have prepared me for the situation I was about to find myself in. I stepped off the plane and down into a black, spiraling abyss. I fell harder and deeper than when I had left the marriage a year before.

There is nothing like a good dose of rejection to get old self-esteem issues rising to the surface. Add into the mix having sex with your rejecter a couple times a week and the fact that he is also hanging out with a twenty-something-year-old girl, and you have the perfect recipe for a complete and utter breakdown. And that is exactly what happened to me. I broke down. What made this all the worse was that each time Brent was with me intimately, he would tell me he loved me, and in my heart I knew it was true. He would also say he couldn't be with me because he couldn't be what I needed, he wasn't ready, and he didn't know how to do the relationship right. Being clairsentient was adding to the hurt. I could feel into him. I knew how much he loved me, I knew he wanted to be with me. I felt his feelings. I knew he was holding back because of his fears, along with the fact that I had been in another relationship. Meanwhile, everyone around me was telling me to stop sleeping with him because I was making things worse for myself. If I stopped sleeping with him, then he'd stop treating me like crap. Again, intuitively I knew exactly what was going on. He was testing me, pushing me away, trying to hurt me, trying to see if I would go away again. I knew I had to stand strong and continue to show him my love. I had to prove I wasn't going anywhere, no matter how hard he tried to prove I would leave again.

I want to add a side note to all this. I am not talking about taking abuse or mistreatment in any way. This was a different situation. Brent truly, deeply loved me and I had torn his entire life apart when I left him. He was scared to death of feeling that kind of pain again, hence the testing and pushing. It was extremely hard to take and hard on my heart.

I couldn't eat, I couldn't sleep, and I couldn't think. For two weeks all I did was cry. I was also really angry at God, His workers, or whoever the hell it was who had told me to come back for him. I thought they were wrong and that I was too late.

Finally, Brent agreed to go with me to counseling with P.T. The problem was he was willing to do his part of the personal work on himself only half the time; the other half, his mid-life crisis alter ego would take over and refuse to do anything. So I did the only thing I could do. I did the work I needed to do for me. Painfully, I looked at all my own fears and insecurities, and looked at and dealt with my beliefs and feelings about being attractive and about aging, about being loved and worthy. I needed to acknowledge my codependent tendencies, my core fear of abandonment, and how I turned my anger inward. I did process after process at home, alone, in my bedroom mirror.

The whole experience, painful as it was, was truly a gift and opportunity for me to look deep into myself, my dark, and my crap, and to clean out as much of it as I could. Although it was long and painful, after two months Brent and I finally reconciled.

As a part of the public statement that we were officially back together, Brent invited me to attend the horsemen's awards banquet with him. I knew his twenty-something *friend*, as he called her, was also going to be there with her boyfriend. So, while I knew my ego was working overtime, I decided I was going to prove that being nearly forty didn't mean I was an over-the-hill washout. I went out shopping for the sexiest, most sultry little dress I could find. I picked myself up a rocking set of stiletto heels to match. By the time I was done I had an outfit to kill. Brent's mouth fell open when I arrived at his door.

Normally I am a very low-key plain Jane, and this is what most of the horsemen who knew me remembered. Most of them hadn't even seen me in the last nine years because I'd stopped having anything to do with the horseracing industry altogether. I changed people's opinions and memories that night. I embraced every aspect of my femininity and my womanness. I called on every energy goddess I knew to support me. I wasn't just doing it for me alone, I was doing it for every woman over thirty-five who had been erased from the "Book of Sexy" merely because of her age. While I had always found this age bias around women's sexuality frustrating, it had hit me hard because of my recent experience with Brent and the young girl. I had a point to prove and prove it I would.

The cut of the dress over-accentuated each curve. I had always had a decent body, but I'd never done anything to draw attention to it before. I figured this was a now-or-never moment.

Brent grinned ear to ear as we strolled through the banquet room. Heads turned everywhere. People weren't sure if I was his ex-wife or if he had hired an escort.

The most memorable moment was when we approached our table. Sitting only a few tables away was Brent's young friend. She caught sight of Brent first and tried to send him a secret smile. Then I moved in beside him and wrapped my hand around his waist. Her eyes were huge as she looked me up and down slowly, assessing every aspect. I was sure, guessing by the look on her face, she was expecting a dumpy, middle-aged housewife. It was a great moment.

The evening ended with a flattering offer from an intoxicated young girl who wanted to take me home. I politely declined, explaining my date wouldn't like that very much. Yes, a lot of ego was involved that evening at the banquet, but after all, I did incarnate as a human, to be human. This was me, totally enjoying my female humanness to its fullest.

Now that Brent and I were back together, we had a lot of work to do on our relationship. We both knew we had stuff to clear from the last couple of years. We both had projections and beliefs that would need to be looked at and processed if we wanted to move forward with each other in a healthy, happy way. Every day we took an hour or more to do a "clearing." We would sit cross-legged, our knees touching, and simply look at one another. We maintained eye contact for at least ten minutes, connecting and watching our thoughts. Then we would begin the process part, which was always the toughest. We each knew we had to be completely willing to hear the other, without taking on anything that was being said. We had to be fully committed to allowing the process of revealing our deepest truths and to hearing the other without judgment. Having the right mindset was vital to the success of the clearing.

We would take turns saying five statements that started with, "What I want you to know is…" and then we'd fill in the rest with something that pertained to ourselves, such as, "I'm scared I can't trust you," or "I feel very vulnerable right now." The other person would then acknowledge each statement with, "Thank you." Back and forth we'd go in rounds of five until we felt completely clear. One of the harder processes was the statement that started with, "What I don't want you to know is…" We did that one every day. Most of us have a tendency to withhold or hide, believing our thoughts or actions are so wrong or bad that we need to keep them from our partner. While that may seem safer, each thing we hide away and do not share first gains power over us, then becomes a small brick in the wall that eventually blocks us completely off from our partner. If Brent and I truly wanted to be together, heart to heart, without baggage or walls between us, then everything needed to be cleared out.

In all of our processing and long evening discussions about relationships, we came across an important discovery. Nearly every relationship will go through what we termed a "fall from grace." Every person comes into a relationship with different hurts and issues from the past. Each of us has a core hurt. It's the big hurt, the big fear. My core issue has always been abandonment. First I felt abandoned by God, then I was abandoned by my father when he took his life. I had lots of smaller issues, but this was the one to trump them all.

In a relationship, at some point, our partner is going to trigger that core issue. All relationships are like mirrors. We have the opportunity to see ourselves, our mind, and our beliefs through our partner. It is the largest opportunity for growth being human provides, if we choose to be conscious and use it that way.

The fall from grace usually happens shortly after the rush of infatuation on first meeting someone begins to level out. At some point, in some way, our new partner is going to trigger our deepest core issue. For me, it was the moment when Brent's mother had made harsh accusations against both me and my six-year-old son Brandon. She called Brent to deliver her disparaging statements and he did nothing but listen to her. He didn't defend either of us and he didn't tell her she had to stop. He said nothing. Of course he had his own reasons, but mainly he still allowed his mother to control him. But I didn't care what his reasons were; that behavior triggered my core issue of abandonment. Brent wasn't there for me when I needed him to be. He didn't have my back, and I could never trust him on a deep level to support me. I felt I was on my own, should anything else happen. I could never rely on him again. That happened about one year into our relationship, and it was Brent's fall from grace in my eyes.

In turn, I had triggered Brent's biggest core issue—his sense that I was controlling—about six months into the relationship. At the time, P.T. and I had a major disagreement, and he told me to leave the community. I was angry about my situation and I gave Brent an ultimatum: stay in the community without me or leave with me and we would remain together. To Brent, the ultimatum was control. Although he desperately wanted to stay, he left the community to be with me. I was never quite the same to him in his eyes after that. I was another person who tried to control him. I had fallen from grace in his eyes.

As we looked back through all of our previous relationships, we saw that the fall from grace had played out each time in different ways. The two of us realized that if a couple were to be conscious of the fall from grace *before* going into a new relationship, it could provide a tremendous opportunity to heal that core issue. We understood that the reason we have the issue play out over and over in the first place is so we can eventually heal it.

Even though we understood each other far better now, we believed that at some point we were going to again come up against each other's core beliefs. We just didn't know when. We were going to have to work hard to remain as conscious as possible with each other now. That way, when the event did come up, we could help each other through it. Of course, as with all personal growth work, it's easier said than done.

Thus, with our new vows of commitment to each other, our relationship, and ourselves, Brent and I remarried. This time, we chose to marry legally, and for the first time, I had a wedding ring on my finger. Brent left the old farmhouse and he and the boys moved into the hippie house with me. Life was good now. I felt like I had a foundation under my feet for the first time in years.

I was inspired to become more involved with my fractal work and to promote the cards. I also began picking up more website jobs. My goal was to hopefully earn enough money that Brent could leave the horseracing industry once and for all.

If an intention is put out into the Universe with enough energy and passion, it usually manifests. Unfortunately for Brent and me, however, the intention to leave the horse business came sooner than we were prepared for. We had just come back from a ten-day budget vacation to Arizona. It was the first vacation Brent had taken in over nine years. His wealthy employer, however, didn't feel the horsemen were entitled to vacations, as they were self-employed contract workers. And regular labor laws didn't apply. Brent was relieved from his position as farm manager within a few days of our return.

To say Brent was devastated was an understatement. He had worked there for over eleven years with a fierce loyalty to the millionaire owner, who had now tossed him out as if he were an empty paper coffee cup. With no skills in anything else but horses, Brent had hit a crisis in his life. He was nearly fifty and felt he had nothing to show for it, and worse, nothing to move forward with. I, on the other hand, was a having a different crisis. This now put me into the role of provider for my family. It was a huge pressure. I had scarcely been able to feed myself when I was alone, and now I was responsible for the wellbeing of my entire family. I did the only thing I could do—I put my nose to the grindstone and started working sixteen-hour days again. I tried to earn enough money to live on while battling the compulsion to give away my work for free.

One positive thing to come of this was our new online store, Soul Vibes Metaphysical. We decided to sell my cards, along with other unique spiritually based products, through a website I would build. I would then connect this store to my own website. Brent would stay home and put his energy into growing a business for us. I would do all the marketing and advertising while he took care of the sales and store management. It was almost ideal for us. Now we could work together at a business that held meaning for us both.

My relationship with Juan and his wife remained strong throughout this time. I would speak with her at least once a week, and our phone calls always brought a smile to my heart. She was like a sister to me now, which is why I was faced with a dilemma when she invited me to visit them in Florida. I couldn't really afford a trip to the southern States. Basically, Juan said I would have free food and lodging while I was there. He figured that since I was so small, I couldn't possibly eat that much rice and beans. I scraped together what little money I had, and with a smile and a blessing, Brent waved goodbye to me.

I had never been to any of the southeastern States before, and I had no concept of what muggy meant until I arrived there. It was like being in a steam room everywhere I went. No matter how much I sweated, my body just couldn't cool itself because the air was so thick with moisture. I felt as if I was suffocating the entire time. It was probably why I had such a hard time one morning as we prepared our small outdoor site for the sweat lodge we would be building.

Juan had been holding traditional Native North American sweat lodge ceremonies for over twenty years. A small hole was dug in the earth to hold the hot rocks, and a teepee-like structure was built over top to contain the heat and steam. Essentially, it was a sacred sauna that helped to purify the body, mind, and soul. A part of the tradition was that the women had to wear long skirts to the ankles. I was happy to honor the tradition, but found it difficult to gather the large rocks and walk with them while in my loose cotton skirt. With the moisture in the air and the sweat that ran down my legs, every stitch of the fabric clung to me. My once loose and flowing skirt turned into a fully constricted kimono, forcing me to walk in baby steps and making the job of collecting rocks that much harder.

I was hot, frustrated, and tired. Every time Juan made eye contact with me he would smile, though I knew he was secretly laughing at the sight of me. More than once he stated something to the effect of, "It makes the Spirit strong!" I'd just walk away, grumbling. I wanted nothing more than to rip that constrictive skirt from my body and take a running dive into the nearest body of water. Because this was Florida, however, I wasn't going within a hundred feet of any water, lest I should be eaten by a pack of crocs. Instead, I continued to work and pushed the thought of a cold, refreshing splash as far from my mind as I could.

It was mid-afternoon by the time everything was ready. Before we bent down to crawl into the lodge, one of the other women threw a warning my way. "Juan makes his sweats hot, you know, so stay low."

I smiled and replied, "It's okay, I've done sweats before." Oh, silly me! I should have asked her how hot, exactly, was hot. I should have asked her if any other humans had survived his sweats besides her. I should have asked her to point to the nearest escape exit so I could make a getaway when I felt the flesh searing off my face.

Never in my life had I been situated in heat like that. The sweats I had done before were certainly hot—that was the point. But this? If one could imagine an inferno or an incinerator, that was what this was like. Each round of gratitude and prayers meant more lava-hot rocks were added inside our little hut. I was nearly turned backward, trying to get my face away from the fiercely hot steam that each toss of water onto the rocks produced. Inhaling the air was like inhaling fire itself. Suddenly, Juan's wife leaned in and whispered to me to lie down. She gently pushed my face into the cool earth. For the first time since entering, I was able to breathe. Shortly after, the first round ended. We were welcome to take a step outside, to gain a reprieve from the heat inside. I quickly crawled around the perimeter to the doorway, desperately in need of some cooler air. My hands and legs were shaking, and my chest was heavy with a lump that had been building inside me. I needed to gather myself, but I felt as though I had only just gotten outside when we were called back in for the second round.

I had always thought I was tough, but I wasn't tough enough for this. I sat on a large rock just outside the entrance. Everyone else made their way back in, but I remained on my rock, breathing and shaking. I simply could not make myself go back inside. I was angry at my weakness. I was angry for dishonoring the gift of this sacred ceremony my brother had given me. I was angry at the heat. I was angry for being angry. I was so angry that I wanted to run far, far away from this place and from myself, but I just sat there immobilized on my rock.

After a few minutes, I heard Juan gently called my name. "Come, Cheryl. Come." He spoke softly from inside as he held the flap of the doorway open.

I began to shake hard now. I had to face him and tell him I could not go back.

"I—I—" The attempt to speak broke my strength and the tears began to roll down my dirty cheeks. My head automatically began to turn from side to side to convey the message my mouth could not. I looked up in his eyes as I sat there crying, shaking, and swinging my head *no.*

Juan bowed his head slightly, to honor what I was trying to say. Then he closed his eyes and motioned me to come back inside.

Still I shook my head. He seemed not to acknowledge me, slowly nodding his head yes, eyes closed, and then he waved me in again.

Both Juan and I were, by nature, fiery people. Somehow he knew that any force or pressure on his part would have sent me high-tailing it out of there faster than a rabbit trying to escape an eagle's descent. Instead, he used the one method I could not resist. He used kindness.

When our eyes met at our third round of yes and no, I saw only love and compassion for me. I saw my resistance clearly in that moment too—my resistance to everything. I saw how I often resisted life itself. I wanted to break through this resistance—I did not want my mind to hold me back from this powerful experience of awareness and potential healing. I dropped my head, took one last large breath of outside air, and made my way on my hands and knees over to my place inside.

Every round brought more rocks, each splash of water brought more steam. I dreamily listened to rounds of prayers spoken in both Spanish and English. I was the only English-speaking person here; everyone else was from South America. I realized they were speaking English only to honor me. That's when my last ounce of resistance broke fully and a rush of love swept through me, bursting my heart wide open. There was so much love that I felt overwhelmed. Tears flowed as I sobbed on the ground, making a little mud puddle where I lay. I'm sure no one even understood my words when my turn for prayer came. Through my heavy breaths and jagged voice I cried my gratitude out to all. It was short and quick. I could barely even think, my emotions were so strong. I just wanted to lie back down on the cool earth so I could purge and release.

With the ceremony completed, we made our way outside. I felt like a new woman as I stood and stretched. I must have looked like disaster, though—covered in dirt, wild, curly hair, and swollen eyes—but I didn't care. I was filled with gratitude for the powerful experience of love and for sticking it out when I wanted to run.

Juan came over to give me a hug. "*Si*, Cheryl, you did it. Yes? Now, the fire? It move and purify from your head and into your heart. *Si*, this is good fire now. Fire in the heart!" I understood what he meant. I had purified the fire of my anger and moved it into my heart, which was now wide open and bursting with love.

"That was beautiful, Juan. Thank you!" I was half laughing and half crying.

It would not be the last powerful healing I would receive through my connection with Juan. I had one more experience to go, but it would be in Sweden and would literally bring me to my knees.

⚜ *16* ⚜

A New Understanding

I had just finished hanging up the phone with Juan and his wife, finalizing our plans. It was the month of January, and in May we would be heading off to Sweden to do some talks. Juan had personally asked me to help promote and manage him. Of course, Juan was the main speaker, but he had asked me to play my video as the opener to his talks. I was more than honored to oblige, happy to do anything that didn't put me in the spotlight.

My beautiful friend Kristina would be organizing most of it in Sweden. I would be making all the flyers and advertisements, as well as new websites for both Juan and Kristina. I had a lot to do and very little time to do it. As usual, I offered to do everything for free. Juan had offered to pay for my ticket to Sweden, but he would pay me after the talks, when he had the money. I didn't have the cash for a ticket either, but I did have a credit card that hopefully had enough room on it for one more charge.

Between putting all the materials together for this event and building websites on the side so my family could eat, I had little time left for marketing and promoting the cards. The big drawback to self-publishing was that I had to come up with thousands of dollars to print the cards. Once they arrived, I had to do everything else required to market and sell my cards. It's not easy to be a one-woman show. I had to admit that the stress of it all was starting to take its toll.

Time alone for meditation and prayer or extra time to play with fractals simply wasn't an option. With Brent working for our company now, he was home all day, every day, which meant I didn't get any time to myself. Yet my sanity came from having space and time to be completely on my own. I did all my best thinking, creating, thought clearing, and emotion processing when I was alone. I was already having a hard time dealing with my massive workload. Being deprived of alone time only made matters worse. I was slowly compressing under the weight of it all.

Just weeks before it was time to depart to Scandinavia, one of the largest volcanic eruptions in recent history shut down the airspace for weeks, leaving travelers stranded all over the globe. Although Iceland was situated high in the northern hemisphere, the ash clouds from the Eyjafjallajökull volcano had spread down as far as middle Europe. All air traffic was at a halt. Kristina and I prayed to the gods of land and air that this situation would clear so we could get on with the event we had now been planning for months.

Six days before my departure, Juan's wife called. She informed me they did not have their visas yet. I felt overwhelmed and helpless. She explained how their time had been limited and this was the first opportunity they'd had. She also explained that this was how the energy of Spirit was moving for them and there was nothing they could do. She did, however, fully reassure me they would have their appointment for their visas in just a couple of days, then they would be on their way.

For residents of certain countries in South America, the visa process is complicated because of the high risk of criminal activities.

All I could do was move forward as planned and trust Spirit would take care of the rest.

Fortunately, flights returned to normal, and I was now on my way to Sweden. I had booked my ticket with Icelandair because the flights were so cheap. It was a good call; I ended up having a lot of cabin space to myself. Even though I enjoyed the flight, I couldn't stop the nagging feeling that I didn't want to be making this journey. I had even told Brent of my misgivings that morning as we drove to the airport. For the first time, I wasn't excited to be traveling. At the time, I thought the issues arose because we didn't have the money for my trip, so I ignored the warnings and put my fears aside. I had no idea these were warnings of what was to come once I arrived at my destination.

I had always loved being with Kristina. Someone I could deeply relate to, she would always listen and smile without judgment no matter what crazy stories I told her. She had an uncanny ability to see the symbolic messages in everyday life. Her mind could decipher things no one else could see. For the first day or two after my arrival, we enjoyed hanging out and relaxing while I recovered from the twelve-hour time difference.

Then the calls from Juan's wife began. The good news was that they had their appointment for the visa. But they were not going to be getting their papers until the day before the first talk. With flights and schedules, they would not be arriving until the night of the talk or the morning after. I was devastated. Months of hard work and planning unraveled. We had over seventy people booked for the talk, three solid days of appointments for readings with Juan, a huge Mayan fire ceremony, and a radio interview. Months of organization was now in chaos.

My conversation with Juan's wife didn't go very well. Needless to say, both of us were upset for our own reasons. I was exhausted from months of overworking and trying to support my family. Now I was jetlagged and facing the fact that we would have to cancel the first half of the schedule. Juan's wife worked away from home and had just arrived back after a full month away. She too was exhausted from being the sole provider for her family. She missed her children and was extremely stressed. If we all weren't suffering from so much tension and overwork, things might not have ended as badly as they did.

At least a half dozen times during our conversation, I told her that the only thing that mattered was our friendship and everything else could be resolved. But she could not hear me—she could not get past the fact I had pointed out they only had one responsibility in all of this, which was to get themselves to Sweden on time. In retrospect, I know I shouldn't have been so hard on her. She had done the best she could. When I tried to explain there was no time to reschedule the events and stated exactly how much money they would lose, she lost her calm manner and tuned out. I now know I shouldn't have mentioned that either, but they *had* asked me to manage everything, and I thought it was important they knew they would be losing over half of their income because of their delay. I tried explaining that it was the single most important event in a major city that week. Still, she didn't understand.

I realized I must have hurt her emotionally, because in our talks that followed, she made accusations that white people were concerned only about money. How "you people," as she put it, were "not in your hearts." She made it clear that they only worked for Spirit, not for money. I knew this was only her anger talking, but it still hurt. And I was bewildered. Had she forgotten that both Kristina and I had been working on this for months now, receiving no compensation along the way? How could she forget I had spent all that time building Juan a polished website so he could spread the word about his work and the Mayan message to humanity? I had done that purely out of the goodness of my heart, and the only compensation I had been promised was my airline ticket to Sweden.

182

Yes, I had hoped I would get some compensation at the end of his talks, but I didn't expect it.

Beyond my own efforts, Kristina had done almost everything else. She had sent out the information and booked the events, the location, the people, and the readings with Juan. She had done it all simply because she wanted to help share the Mayan message. She had even put up her own money and was allowing all of us to stay in her little apartment, yet she had asked for absolutely nothing in return. I said nothing of this to Juan's wife, but I wanted to.

Subdued a little, I tried telling her none of this really mattered. They could still come and do the other talks and readings for the people. If they were working for Spirit, then Juan still had a great opportunity to share his message with everyone. They didn't have to worry about the money part; I promised I wouldn't mention it again. I appealed to her, saying the only thing truly important was our friendship, but it was to no avail. She was angry and they were now not coming.

To say I was crushed didn't even begin to describe how I felt. She had been one of my best friends for over two years, and our friendship was over because of this? I couldn't believe it. Was such a petty monetary issue a reason to turn your back on someone you love? I valued nothing more than my relationships with the people I loved. I always held a strong belief that people could work through any problem, because that's what friendship was about.

It was such a disaster that I immediately fell into a black hole, crying and sobbing for two days straight. Kristina held it together like a champion. With the efficiency of a professional, she proceeded to cancel events and notify people. That isn't to say she wasn't affected—she was devastated for her own reasons. But by the third day, she broke down too. What a pair we were—unshowered, in our pajamas, and crying all the time. Soiled tissues littered the small coffee table.

It was time to get to the bottom of the issues and figure out exactly what part I had played in all this. I had to examine my triggers, my anger, and my pain, turning everything inside out. If there was one thing I knew, it was that I wanted to understand this lesson now. I never wanted to go through something like this again.

Fortunately, Kristina had done a lot of personal growth work similar to what I had learned. Together we were able to help each other see through our projections and pain, into the core of the issue. That kind of introspection was always hard, but by the fourth day I felt fairly clear about what had really happened.

Juan was not the first older man I had helped to promote for free and with whom it had ended badly. I began to see that it could be a father issue for me. I was trying to freely give away my love, my time, and everything else I had. In the end, none of it was valued, and they left. There was that abandonment issue again. For the first time, I also saw clearly how I was constantly doing things for others so I could prove once and for all that I was a good person. Subconsciously, I was still trying to prove I wasn't the "detriment to society" they had labeled me all those years ago. Whatever I had to do to prove they were wrong about me, I'd do it. I was continuing to work until my fingers bled and just giving it all away. The fact that I suffered by never having enough to get by on made it that much better; I was unwittingly punishing myself for whatever my wrongdoings were in the past. My instinctual nature to help others had been hijacked by my ego. It wasn't serving me or the world in the way it had been intended to. I had to claim this part of myself back.

The insight went even deeper. I saw how I had been doing this for years. Even Brent had pointed out how I would quickly take on anyone's project or work to help them, throwing my own work to the side. This was a deflection. I would keep myself busy with good deeds, so to speak, so I didn't have to work on walking my own path in life. Surely it would be okay with Spirit if I didn't walk my own path, because clearly they could see all the good I was doing instead!

I saw all my beliefs about money, myself, men, and life reveal themselves to me. I knew I still had a long way to go in valuing myself and what I had to offer the world. Although my heart ached over the loss of my friendship with Juan and his wife, at least I was clear about why it had happened. I would actually mourn the loss of them for many more months to come. For now, I was at least able to hold my head up straight.

Both Kristina and I were embarrassed at having been accused of being money mongers and heartless white people. We decided to tell everyone that Juan had not been able to come for personal reasons. By day six I felt strong enough to face the world once again. If I was feeling leery, I could only imagine how poor Kristina felt. I didn't live here and it wasn't my personal circle of friends that I had to face. I admired her strength and I knew when she joked about being a strong Nordic woman that she wasn't really joking.

But fate was not finished with me yet, and a beautiful soul named Ingela invited me to talk at her healing center. She had originally booked the full Mayan event, but Spirit called her to have me talk on my own, regardless. She and Kristina were very good friends; she was fully aware of what had really happened with Juan.

Ingela's center was called Mötesforum Futura and was situated in the countryside of Gärds Köpinge, a two-hour drive away. Kristina had raved about the energy of Ingela's center, but it wasn't until I experienced it myself that I had any idea how profound it was. As we turned off the main road, we headed down a long dirt drive that cut straight through farmland. It was magical. The left-hand side was lined with a dense row of trees. An old stone fence ran along their base. I could only imagine how long ago that short stone wall had been built. After a couple of minutes, the road ended and we arrived at our destination. This property was even more magical than what we had just driven through. The healing center was housed in a new structure on the property, and the rest of the buildings were charming and rustic with that old European look and feel. The trees nestled along the end of the property line, where a wide, calm stream flowed. I was surrounded by nothing but nature and beauty. No longer able to contain my delight, I started to squeal out. Oh, how my heart needed this. I looked up to the sky and offered a silent prayer of gratitude.

Ingela arrived shortly after us. I loved her the moment I met her. Her sparkling eyes reflected the purity of her soul. She was grounded and loving, with a wide-open heart. We were the first overnight guests, and she was excited to show us the rooms in the center. I was amazed. The entire center had been colored with prayer-infused, ecological paint made with herbs and plants. Symbolic artwork decorated the walls throughout. Each room, complete with its own ensuite, represented a chakra and was designed to activate and heal that particular energy center. The main living room had floor-to-ceiling windows that offered a peaceful view of the stream and property.

I found it no coincidence that Ingela had decided I would be staying in the blue room, representing the throat chakra. Her intuition proved accurate that this was truly the best choice for me.

I hadn't done a talk now in almost two years. Added to that was the fact that my computer had contracted a virus just a few days before. My computer was my entire professional life, and it held the files to the slideshow I usually used during my talks. Even though I considered myself a computer nerd, for the life of me I was not able to remove the virus myself as I usually did, and I didn't have the money to get it fixed. I didn't know it at the time, but the Universe was slowly stripping away everything I identified with. First it was my exuberant generosity in giving, then my computer, which held every facet of the work I did. Then it was down to the little things such as my toothpaste, which I had an allergic reaction to, and the fact that I had forgotten both my Blackberry charger and my curling iron before we left for Ingela's. Now I had no e-mail contact at all, I couldn't talk with Brent, whom I leaned on heavily for emotional support, and I couldn't brush my teeth or even tame my naturally wild hair.

Perhaps to someone else it wouldn't seem like much, but these were some of the most vital things to me in my life. Everything I strongly identified with had been taken away. The night before my talk, I was nearing an emotional breakdown, but not wanting to look pathetic and weak, I tried to keep it inside.

That evening, Kristina and I headed across the yard to have dinner at Ingela's as usual. After a marvelous salmon dinner, the three of us dove into a hearty discussion led by Ingela. Innocently, she explained her view of the different roles we play in life and in the lives of others. As she moved to the part about communication, I began to believe she was covertly trying to send me a message about how I should speak and what I should and should not be sharing. Of course, that wasn't the message she was really trying to convey, but at the time, my mind perceived it that way. As she spoke, she drew little diagrams, and all the while I grew more and more upset inside.

Finally, I could take no more and I started to defend myself. She didn't understand what was going on with me, and she tried to explain her meaning. But all I was getting out of her words was that I needed to be careful about what I shared and that not everyone would be ready to hear what I had to say. In other words, I didn't know how to do it right. I was going to make mistakes and fail at the talk altogether.

I ended up bursting into tears and running back to our room. For nearly an hour I cried on my bed, feeling like the entire world was against me. I didn't want to do the talk and I didn't want to be here. I wanted the shoulder of my husband to cry on. I wanted desperately just to disappear, to be back at home where I could hide. I was also angry I had come here in the first place. Why had my heart told me to come, despite the fact that it hadn't felt good? I couldn't make sense of it.

Feeling frustrated and very tired of crying, since I had cried during most of this visit to Sweden, I pulled myself from my bed and headed outside for a smoke. Out here in the solitude of the country, there was no sound but the faint rushing of the stream. The air was still cold, but it was refreshing on my eyes, which were swollen once again. I continued to sit there, eyes closed, squatting up against the side of the building, long after the cigarette was done.

That is when it all unfolded, like a new lotus flower blossoming on a warm summer's day. Suddenly, I saw the whole picture of everything that had transpired and why. It was an elaborate plan to strip me of everything so I could finally see who I was really was. There was nothing left to hide behind—hiding was all I had ever done. It was time for me to be who I really was. It was time for me to show my heart, unprotected and open, to the world. I needed to allow my own voice to be heard. I had to trust the Universe and this strange path I was on. It was time for me to draw from my own source of power within. I understood the great lengths the Universe had gone to to help me see the light. My work, my path, was the most important thing in my life, and I had to finally claim that while remaining as open and as honest as I could. That is how I would shine my Light.

The next morning I was quick to make my way over to Ingela's house to apologize for my behavior the night before. I thanked her for her part, as it was exactly what I'd needed. She, in return, offered me a free session before my talk later that afternoon. I was happy to accept. I knew Ingela's work involved psychology and the different brain hemispheres. Using those tools, she helped people to move forward in their lives and on their paths. I also knew she was extremely intuitive, but I didn't realize how tuned in she really was until our session.

She had said my power was like a tiger, but I feared the tiger and kept it caged. She explained it was time to let it out and allow it to walk with me, beside me in life. This completely made sense as I thought back a few days. While we visited Kristina's friend, his Egyptian healing cat, which was just days away from giving birth, had jumped onto my back. Her friend was surprised at the cat's behavior, as she had never done that before. However, during healing circles, she would come and lie in the laps of those who needed healing. She was tabby in color, with tiger stripes. What Ingela said made perfect sense now.

"Cheryl," Ingela spoke softly and firmly, "you also have to claim your space and your part in the work you do."

"I do, Ingela, so I don't get what you mean."

"No dear, you don't. You push your work out in front of you, wanting the work to represent itself, yes? But you do not realize you are the one bringing this work forth into the world. Without you, it would not be what it is." She caught me trying to look away, knowing this was hard for me to hear. She reached out and put a hand on my arm to get me to make eye contact again. "Cheryl, you are the one the Universe has chosen to do this work. *You.* Therefore, *you* must stand tall and represent both the work and yourself to the world. You are just as much of an important factor as the cards themselves. Trust the Universe in their choice. The more you show of yourself, the more power and energy you give to the work itself."

That was it, I was crying again. She had hit the one last spot I had failed to see for myself—me. And most importantly, it all went right along with what I had seen for myself last night. I knew in my heart it was all true. It was truly time for me to step into the world.

I took everything Ingela offered me and the insights I had gained on my own. My talk at Ingela's went far better than I had imagined it would. I hid nothing. I showed my deepest self as a part of what I do, instead of only the fractal work I did. I was humble yet honest, and I put my heart out there, unprotected. At the end, we played Kristina's copy of my *Greatest Mystery* video. I waited outside the room. When it was done, Kristina directed everyone over to the main center for soup. Afterwards, we held a Shamanic sound healing with Kailash Kokopelli. One after another, each person came out of the room. Nearly everyone was in tears and wanted a hug. They had been touched deeply, not just by the video, but because of the honesty and love that I had shared. Their response had touched me deeply. I had never been so open or vulnerable with a group of people before, and for the first time that felt emotionally and spiritually real. I was proud to be me. I was proud of myself for finally letting down all my guards and allowing myself to be seen by others.

I walked around outside while everyone inside was enjoying the soup. I needed a couple of moments alone to process what had happened. As I came around the side of the center, there was Kailash tending a large fire. It had been strategically placed in front of the living room window of the healing center, so that we could all watch the fire as we ate. When Kailash caught sight of me he called me over.

"I would like a moment of your time, if that's okay?" Kailash asked. He wasn't a big man, and if I didn't know better I might have thought he was a true Native American. Kailash was a very gentle soul. He was deeply spiritual and had traveled wide and far, living with many of the world's different indigenous tribes and spiritual leaders. I respected and admired him.

"I have time for you, Kailash, for sure." I offered a smile as I approached. It wasn't until I came closer that I saw tears streaming down his face. Out of respect, I remained quiet, until he was ready to speak.

"Cheryl," he said, slowly lifting his eyes away from the fire to look into mine, "I have met many, many people who claim to be spiritual. Many of them are very learned in certain traditions and they know many things. Yet I have only met a few people who are truly spiritual and wise. You, my sister, are one of those people."

The depth of his words and the sincerity of his tone had touched me deeply. I was speechless. I simply stood there allowing myself to take it all in.

"Your heart is pure. You are honest and humble. You did not try to tell anyone anything. You simply shared of yourself, your love, and your Light, and every one of us here has received from that, including me. And I thank you."

I used this opportunity to give Kailash the biggest hug I had to give. It took everything within me not to cry. All these years, I had fought so hard to hide and believed I had nothing to offer personally—being me wasn't quite good enough for the world. Now I saw that those beliefs were nothing but lies. I most certainly did have something to offer this world. It was the one thing I had that no one could take, yet anyone could have. What I had to offer was my heart and my love, and it was enough.

We finished the night with one of the most astounding sound healing experiences I had ever had. The more time passed, the more I witnessed what a gifted man Kailash Kokopelli was. By the end of the evening, everyone who had come left serene and smiling. Both Kailash and I had honored ourselves and our gifts, sharing them with everyone here, and I saw the benefits of that sharing directly. Finally, I really understood.

In all, my time in Sweden was one of the most insightful and life-changing experiences I'd had yet. I was coming home with a whole new perspective of myself and my work and I was going to do my best to honor both. To Juan and his wife, I sent my prayers many times over for the vital role they had played in the gift I had received here. With my faith in myself restored, I was now going to take my work to a whole new level and put myself in the spotlight like never before. It wouldn't be long before my faith in Spirit would be put through the ultimate test. I was just about to experience not only one of the most terrifying events of my life but also one of the greatest miracles a person could ever witness.

⚬ *17* ⚬

The Power of a Miracle

With my passion renewed for my work and a heightened awareness that I needed to put myself at the forefront, I dove headfirst into the fractals and the cards. I also began to wean off all my web design clients. That was a big leap of faith, as it had been our main source of bread and butter up to this point. I figured if Spirit really meant what I had learned, then I would be fully taken care of. And I was.

Within a month of putting my heart and soul into my work, things began to really take off. Of course, our income had dropped considerably without the website work, and some months I wondered if I was going to have to get a part-time job somewhere. I just held on tight and kept my nose to the grindstone. Where the cards had only really been known in North America all these years, suddenly, the world was starting to take an interest. I'm not sure if I was more surprised or delighted.

I decided to have a stronger presence on Facebook. I already had a fan page for the cards and an application where Facebook users could play with them. There again, I had struggled with allowing myself to be seen and allowing my real voice to be heard. Up until that point, I had been content with posting a few fluffy little quotes as the status of the fan page. I had struggled with the belief that I would offend people if I voiced my own words and opinions. Now I began using my own quotes, but I tried to keep them tame. They were still often more fluff and bubbles than anything. Suddenly, someone began to take me to task for a small statement I'd made about what I believed, which happened to go against the norm of the New Age community. After a couple of argumentative posts from that person, my old fighting spirit kicked in. This time, though, it wasn't anger. It was just the extra dose of attitude I needed to finally post what I really thought. The next day I carefully wrote out the status for the fan page wall. I held my breath and hit the button to make it public.

"If I wanted to conform to society's idea of what to believe, how to walk my Path, and how to connect to God, then I would have incarnated as a sheep! But since I didn't, I am going to take full advantage of this human incarnation. I will stand tall in who I am. I will live free. I will stay true to me and not give up anything just to please someone else. Most importantly, I will be all that I am and can be, while I am here."

I was anxious as I awaited the reaction. I felt frightened, taking a stand like this, but it was a matter of principle now. No matter how much fear I felt, I would now always stand up for what I believed in. The response from the fans was overwhelming. It was as if the wall had really come alive for the first time. People loved it. One person even commented how he had no taste for the candy-coated stuff and this was exactly what he wanted to read.

It was time for me to let go of yet another false belief. I no longer had to hold my voice back; as long as I spoke with honesty and it was my truth, it was okay to share. Such a small incident had provided me with a very big lesson.

With the sudden boom of interest in my work, one of the benefits was that we began to sell more of my destiny cards than ever before. This was both good news and bad news. We didn't have a penny to put toward another print run and we were nearly out of cards. We needed to come up with thousands of dollars—and fast. No bank would give us a loan because our monthly income was too little. None of our friends had that kind of money lying around. For weeks I was stressed about it, not knowing what to do. Then one day, I thought of the one place we could get the money—a forbidden source. This money was never to be touched, and we struggled for days over the dilemma. Finally, we decided: Brent and I were going to cash in Jaden's education savings plan. I thought it was the right decision, until we actually did it. Then I broke down.

I had only one major dream as a teen and adult, and it was to go to university. Since I never could, it was important to me that I provide my son with that option. Now I was taking it away from him, and the guilt was consuming me. But my girlfriends were right there to help me through it. It was the only way. I prayed and begged to my Guides that no matter what happened with the cards in the end, they had to help me restore Jaden's education fund. I had to trust they would.

Even with the money at hand, this print run turned out to present major hurdles. I had worked with this printer before, knowing it was one of the best in the industry. Regardless, problem after problem ensued. Our first date for completion came and went, yet we were no closer to having cards than when we had started. The intensity of the situation grew from bad to worse when we had sold our last deck with no new cards yet on the horizon. The pressure was building. People wanted cards, my distributors wanted cards, and there was nothing I could do about it. Finally, even though it was now several months late, I received a small advance of decks by courier. The remainder would be shipped by boat. Unfortunately, when I received the advance decks, they were far below the quality and standards I had come to expect from this printer. I felt I had to turn the rest of the cards away. Brent was not happy with my decision, however, and we had a big disagreement.

He felt the cards weren't so bad that we couldn't sell them. But my integrity meant everything to me. I would not now—or ever— compromise that for anyone or anything. I didn't care if people would be angry. I didn't care if we didn't have a penny to our names right now. I'd rather starve than accept something I knew not to be right. I was sticking to my guns on this one; I honored these cards and the messages they contained. This was Spirit's work and Spirit's gift to the world. It was my job to ensure that it manifested to the world with the highest of intentions and integrity. Four thousand decks were getting burned whether or not we could pay our rent.

Once again, my faith in my work and in Spirit began to waiver. With everything going so terribly wrong, I thought perhaps I had misunderstood, and I wasn't supposed to be making the cards anymore. I desperately needed outside help to see this clearly and felt as though I needed a reading. The only problem was that no one was very good at reading me. Bizarre as it may sound, most intuitives got lost in a strange spiraling energy and that would be it. The other issue was that most readers around here already knew me, so I always ended up getting their opinions instead of a reading. It was frustrating.

My Guides weren't going to leave me doubting them and my work for long. My girfriend Tracey told me I needed to speak with a woman in the United States named Atira. She insisted that this woman was better than any of the psychics who were writing books or on stage right now. She had no idea why this woman wasn't famous for what she did. I deeply trusted and valued Tracey's opinion, so I went ahead and booked an appointment. Just to be sure, I booked it using my first name and Brent's last name. Since I used my maiden name on all my work, this woman would have no idea who I really was. Hopefully, my reading would remain clean and unbiased.

I was both excited and anxious. It had been a long time since I'd had a reading, and I sure hoped it was worth her fees. I was spending money that could have been put to more practical uses.

At exactly ten o'clock I dialed the number that had been provided in the e-mail. Sure enough, a friendly voice on the other end answered. After a cordial introduction, Atira began to lay out the ground rules for the one-hour reading.

"I'm going to start telling you what I'm picking up," she began. "All I want from you is a yes or a no. Yes, you understand, or no, you don't. I don't want to hear your story. I don't want you to tell me anything. Just let me tell you what hits I am getting and if you understand them, okay?"

Jackpot! This is the kind of reading I'd been looking for, and I couldn't wait to get started. She also explained some basics about energy and her readings. I giggled and told her there was nothing that could happen during our reading that was too strange for me. Finally, we got underway.

"Boxes," she began. "I see boxes and boxes everywhere...but you aren't moving. What are these boxes? Don't answer that. Do you understand these boxes?"

"Yes!" I replied enthusiastically. I was giddy with excitement. Of course I knew those boxes—they were my cards. We were off to a great start!

"Great. Okay. Now there are angels... a *lot* of angels. I see twenty-two of them around you. Okay, okay. Around the end of May, beginning of June, something major happened for you. A breakthrough. It was a major life event that changed your insight or perspective on things. These angels were there supporting you, helping you through this. You understand?" She was speaking quickly now.

I tried to fight the tears, but it was to no avail. I was astonished that she had picked up on my experiences in Sweden. "Yes," I managed to croak out.

196

"Okay, woo…where are you taking me? Woo…oh, I'm way out here. Okay. Now I'm sitting inside the Hubble telescope looking out into the galaxy. Why am I here?" She paused a moment. "I'm slowly spinning around in the Hubble telescope…"

I started to freak out. Just last week I'd begun to meditate again. But every time I meditated, I found myself out in space, with the stars and planets revolving around me. This had happened a half dozen times. "I understand!" I interjected.

She went on to talk about physical symptoms I had been having, which no one but Brent knew about. I was thoroughly impressed. She explained why they were happening and what to do about them.

"Woo…I am way far out here! I've worked in a lot of realms, girl, but I have never been here before! Wow. Okay." She hesitated for a moment before she spoke again. "You're an ambassador of sorts, aren't you? You know you are! These Beings are beyond the angelic realm. It's a mix of sorts—angelic and extraterrestrial—I've never encountered them before. But you're definitely an ambassador for them. Oh, but you won't tell anyone because you think people will think you're crazy. Ha! They are telling me to tell you that you are far from crazy, honey. Far from it. You have to accept your role, regardless of whether you ever tell another soul. Do you understand that? You need to accept this."

This remarkable woman on the phone had just revealed the biggest secret that I kept—the angelic star beings. She had never encountered these Beings before, yet she had described with amazing accuracy what their energy was like, what their message was, and who they were. She had nailed it! I knew beyond a doubt she was not only the real deal, but her gift reached far beyond what most other readers were capable of.

I had to acknowledge her, but I was having a hard time talking. "I completely understand," I whimpered into the phone.

"You're scared of the spotlight," she continued. "This throat chakra of yours…wait a minute! You already *are* in the spotlight.

Oh, you have a hard time with this. I hear them. They're telling me you had better get used to it, because there's more to come. More to come! You have to allow your voice, okay? You have to accept your role here, okay?"

Was there anything Atira could not see? In the end, she answered every question I had written down before I had the chance to ask it. She verified that I was indeed still on the right path and I was doing exactly the right thing. I had also been right about my spiritual support team. It did not matter where the message came from; what was important was the message itself and the fact that I shared it with whoever needed it.

Just as Atira has predicted, the next run of cards turned out perfect. Finally we were stocked and selling once again. Things were rolling along and everything finally felt right in my world. But there was something else that Atira did not see. I fully believe I wasn't supposed to receive a warning about what was to come in two months' time.

Christmas was around the corner now, and Brent and I were frantically busy with sales. More and more countries in the world were now aware of the cards and my work. Australia had sold hundreds of decks in just a couple of weeks. I could scarcely keep up with the daily e-mails I received. I never dreamed things would take off like this. The cards, the energy of the fractal images, and the powerful messages of inspiration they delivered resonated with people everywhere.

It was now Tuesday, December 7th, 2010, and Brent and I had been running around all day. On our way home for dinner, I told him about the new car I wanted. I had just finished reading the last book in the *Twilight* series, where I'd read about my dream car, the Mercedes Guardian. It was missile-proof, flame-proof, and of course, had bulletproof glass. This vehicle could even drive through a forest fire because it had its own oxygen supply. On and on I went about this car, which was safer than any other vehicle on the planet.

Although its price tag was in the hundreds of thousands of dollars, I figured a girl was still allowed to dream. Little did I know that I was energetically picking up on what was about to occur just a few hours later, when we headed back out the door that evening.

It was a typical west coast winter night. The cold ocean air was blanketed with a thick, heavy rain. We were on our way to pick up Jaden and his friend from archery class after having done a quick trip to the mall for some Christmas shopping. Looking to avoid any heavy traffic, we decided to take a back road that had very few houses. This quieter street led directly through an industrial area that was nearly barren except for long rows of warehouses on the right-hand side. We were looking forward to a quiet ride.

It was disappointing to find that the road was quite busy. As we approached one of the major intersections, we were met by a line of cars all making a right-hand turn. The traffic lights were blacked out from a power outage and nearly invisible. There was little to warn the motorists they weren't working except a row of pylons forcing vehicles to detour to the next street down to make their right turn, which was many blocks away. So much for the quiet drive.

Brent continued straight ahead, following other anxious drivers who were now searching for an alternate street on which to make their right turn. I wasn't paying much attention, just gazing out the window dreamily. I was only half aware that we had begun to slow as a long line of cars made their way into the right lane to turn. But we were not turning and would be taking the main road all the way to the end. We angled over into the left lane to drive on through.

I watched as other motorists, who were once ahead of us, completed their right-hand turn and drove away. Then I noticed a car approach from a side street on our right, but I didn't think anything of it. I looked away to fiddle with the radio for a moment. When I looked back up, all sense of peace and safety vanished. I was filled with horror to see the car on the side street now approaching us at a tremendous speed. I screamed at Brent, "They're not stopping!"

He slammed his foot on the brake as the rogue vehicle flew out in front of us.

At that point my normal perception of time changed. Suddenly, everything slowed and a great mental clarity ensued. I was acutely aware of all things happening at once. My husband's lower body was straight and stiff as he attempted to command our car to a stop. His arms were tensed and his knuckles white as he gripped the wheel. The car crossing our path, which had first appeared to be doing about seventy kilometers per hour, now seemed to be moving as if in a movie, in slow motion for dramatic effect. Inch by painful inch I watched it creep slowly across our path. And just as slowly—too slowly—I felt our vehicle's speed diminishing.

In that moment, when we were less than a foot away from the back end of the gray-blue steel blur, something changed. My outstretched hand reached for the dash to help prepare for impact when the interior of our car suddenly seemed brighter. This had happened to me on a few occasions before, when there was something Spirit wanted me to pay attention to. Everything suddenly became fluorescent or luminescent, as if there was more light and color entering my retina than is normally possible. And in this moment, I experienced a kaleidoscope of brilliant color around me. Spirit was definitely here. I was instantly awash with utter calm. Every thought, emotion, and cell in my body was filled with the knowledge and sensation that everything was okay. It was all going to be okay. It was a welcome reprieve from the fear that had been pulsing through me just seconds before. It felt as though the calm lasted for minutes, but I know it was really only moments.

With a sudden *thud* I was jolted back to reality. Time returned to its regular count, and the interior of the car was dim again with only the dash lights glowing. We came to a complete stop on impact, and although we had been thrown forward, neither of us appeared to be injured. *Wow*, I remember thinking, *that wasn't nearly as bad as I thought it would be.*

My thought was interrupted by the explosive sound of metal impacting metal. In an instant, from the oncoming lane of traffic to our left, what seemed to be a freight train running at full steam slammed into the crossing vehicle. And in less than a second, the horrific vision of crunching gray-blue metal flew past me and out of my line of vision. Shock filled my mind as it registered what had happened. A semi truck coming from the opposite direction of us had just slammed into the other side of the gray-blue station wagon at full speed.

Adrenaline pulsated wildly through my body as my husband's words rang in my ears: "Oh my God—they're *dead*!" I was sick with panic and fear. We quickly pulled off the road and out of what we now realized to be a main intersection. Here, four traffic lights sat shrouded in darkness, rendered useless by the power outage.

I screamed at Brent for his phone before rushing from the car. The calm reassurance that everything was okay just moments before disappeared as the dark scene ahead took hold of my mind. As I raced toward the gray-blue car, each step jolted me and I fought my shaking arm to keep the cell phone to my ear. "Police, ambulance, or fire?" asked the confident voice.

"All of them!" I shrieked. The voice on the other end calmly took control and began to extract the information they needed from me.

As I approached the once shiny blue-gray station wagon, I saw that it was nothing more than a heap of twisted metal on the grassy sidewalk. It now faced the same direction we had been heading. The massive eighteen-wheeler that had chewed this car up had carried it through the intersection before spitting it out. The car had spun helplessly back over the road, finally landing on the soft grass. A woman was on her knees looking under the rear tires. Other motorists who had involuntarily witnessed the violent collision also came running.

The woman who had been on her knees rose and began to speak

over the screams that have been etched into my mind forever. She looked at me, pointing down to the ground, and spoke in an eerily calm voice. "That's my daughter, she's under there. My daughter is under the car." My heart jumped as the words slammed into my chest. I looked down to see a child's tiny bottom clad in pink sweat pants. The child was not more than four or five years old, guessing from her size. She was bent in half, her head between her legs, and her short pink shirt was crinkled up, exposing her bare back. The axle of the car sat directly on top of her spine. Scream after scream filled the air. It was loud, much louder than the large number of people who were now gathering, louder than the torrential, cold rain that steadily slammed into the pavement, and much louder than the 911 operator on the other end of the phone.

Shock kicked in. It over took my body and mind with sudden ferocity. My legs began to tremble, my stomach knotted and twisted, forcing me to bend over slightly as my heart broke into pieces. Waves of heaving tears escaped me. *A child? Oh dear God…a child! Under the car! How could this be?* The pain in my heart consumed me and my mind flooded with questions for the only ones who could hear them—my Guides and angels. Then my eyes followed the mother, who was now reaching into the back seat. She was yelling a name and pleading that they wake up. More pain crushed my heart as my eyes adjusted and a vision emerged through the darkness. Still buckled into the car seat was the tiny body of a toddler. Her head lay limp to the side. And although she was secured in the middle of the back seat, the mangled side of the car was nearly touching her where it had crumpled from the impact of the semi truck.

I couldn't take any more. I began a heaving cry that I couldn't control and I couldn't stop. It was like a hideous nightmare, only there was no waking up. *How could this happen? Why would this happen? What had I thought or done to manifest this in my reality?* My eyes burned from the hot tears against the cold winter air, but it was nothing compared to the burning in my heart for these children.

202

Brent had found me and took the phone, as I had been rendered nearly useless. Years of being a first-aid instructor and riding as a third on ambulances in my early twenties, meant absolutely nothing now. I couldn't even tell the 911 operator my phone number, let alone administer first aid. Approaching a scene as the help is much different than being on the scene needing help.

At least ten minutes had passed, and numerous paramedics and fire trucks were now arriving. A swarm of rescue workers took command of the scene, relieving the many good Samaritans who had come to assist. It took just a short time for the crew of trained professionals to do what none of us could. They lifted the crumpled heap of metal and released the child from her deathtrap. It was only then that the screams finally faded.

At this point, Brent and I were directed back to our car to wait. As we reached our SUV, I turned to watch as they lifted the child who had been pinned beneath the wreck, strapped her onto a spine board, and carried her into the awaiting ambulance. I tipped my face up to the sky, my palms facing the same direction. I called every entity I could think of to come and assist in this situation. I felt a powerful surge of energy as I called for the divine Light of God to assist these children and to fill them with Light and love. The flow of healing energy was intense in my body, heightened, I believe, because of the adrenaline and altered state of mind I was in.

Once inside the car, I began an inner dialog with my guardians. *Why would you tell me it was okay if it wasn't okay?! What kind of setup is this?* Now that the initial nightmare was over, my anger kicked in. *Don't tell me I agreed to this experience before I came here because I would never voluntarily sign up for this! God, you guys! And why say it was okay only to take it all back? I am pissed! You'd better make sure those kids are okay!* Oh, the children...my heart panged again and the tears started to flow once more.

An emergency medical helicopter had been called in to take the little girl to the children's hospital downtown. The toddler was taken by ambulance to a local hospital. It was a long, cold, and tiring night of giving statements to the police and investigators.

Once we had picked up Jaden and were back at home, neither Brent nor I could sleep. Over and over we reviewed what happened, what should have happened, why we thought it happened, and how we wished it had never happened. And as we painfully replayed our nightmarish experience the phone rang. It was now 11:45 p.m. Surprised that someone would be calling us this late, we ran to answer it. An officer on the other end had an important question he needed answered. Just before he was ready to let me go he said, "By the way, you were asking all night how the children were. Well, I wanted to let you know we just received an update." A long pause ensued before he continued. "The toddler is fine and is already home. And the little one under the car, well...she has a cut lip!" He half chuckled, but only out of relief. "She's just being kept for observation overnight."

"Oh my God!" It was the best reply I could think of. "She was hit by a force equal to a freight train, thrown out of the window of a moving vehicle, then pinned under a ton of steel for over ten minutes with an axle crushing her spine, and all she has is a cut lip?" I couldn't contain myself, so I didn't. "That is divine intervention. That's a true miracle!"

The officer replied, "Well, in this case, I would have to agree you one hundred percent. It *is* a miracle."

For the next few days I continued to be almost numb with shock, and I would burst into tears unexpectedly and often. I had never before experienced trauma in this way. The accident was plastered all over the news, and I was grateful that we didn't receive the local paper, as I didn't want to read about it. I was amazed at the miracle, but perplexed as to the how or why. The whole experience had affected me deeply.

Within a week, the insurance company informed us that our vehicle was a complete write-off. It was so badly damaged from the crash, that it was no longer safe to drive. I didn't understand how this could be. Neither Brent nor I were injured, and it had only felt like a bump when we impacted. I couldn't believe that our car had suffered that much damage. I was overwhelmed with gratitude for the experience of this powerful miracle and to those divine Beings who had insured the safety of us all. As I sat in my office one morning trying pointlessly to work, the entire meaning of this miraculous event became crystal clear. The main reason I was involved in this accident was so I could learn to have absolute faith. In the moments leading up to the accident when I saw the brilliant colors, my Guides had told me that everything was going to be okay, and I felt that was true. Yet the moment I stepped out of our vehicle, I began to believe my eyes and ears instead of my heart. My mind was telling me everything was not okay. And it truly looked like it wasn't.

What if I had stepped out of my car maintaining the feeling and message from Spirit that everything was going to turn out well? What if I had held that energy strong in my heart, regardless of what was happening around me? How would I have reacted then? Every step and every breath would have been filled with faith. What would have been different, if I had been different?

I didn't know the answer, but I saw clearly how those ideas pertained to every other moment of my waking life—how I always *first* believed in the reality of this world and what my five senses told me. I was being asked to operate in a different way now. I had been shown a miracle. I had to trust God first. I was being asked to walk through life carrying the strength and confidence of Spirit in my heart, no matter what happened in the world around me.

I was astounded. How could I not have seen this until now? I was so moved and so inspired that I decided I had to write about it. I needed to tell the world about this miracle that had occurred and the message it contained. Maybe it would help to encourage others to also have absolute faith.

I carefully composed my story of the accident and placed it on my website's blog section. I poured every ounce of heart and emotion that I could muster into the words. I hoped to connect people to the story and to have them experience it as strongly as I had that night. Since the blog was also linked to my new personal fan page on Facebook, over a thousand people read the story within an hour. Nearly everyone had been touched by it. So many people felt deeply connected to this miracle I had shared.

I knew then that it was finally time for me to do some serious writing. For the last two and a half years, Tracey had been telling me that Spirit wanted me to write. She was an intuitive reader too, and although she didn't do readings for me anymore, Spirit had used her to convey that message. She often gifted me blank journals, hoping to encourage me to begin.

I knew better now. I didn't even bat an eye. There was no more room for *I can't, I'm not ready,* or *I'm not good enough* in my thoughts. It was time for me to write. Not to anyone's surprise but my own, the book completed itself on paper within three short weeks. The only problem was that it didn't have a conclusion. It left me asking, "And so...? What does it all mean? What's this all for?" That night I lay in bed and talked to my Guides, as I did every night before sleeping. This time I questioned the ending to the book I had written. *What was this all for?* I questioned them repeatedly, and just as I was about to drift off, the entire answer flooded into my mind at once. I bolted upright in a flash.

Oh my God, that's it! Thank you! I was so excited that I wanted to tell Brent, but he was sleeping so peacefully beside me that I didn't have the heart to wake him. So I snuggled into the blankets and closed my eyes again. I reviewed the answer I had been given, over and over in my mind, so I wouldn't forget. With peace in my heart, I drifted off to sleep.

That night, when I saw a vision of one fruit standing out from among all the others in the orchard, I understood completely. The nature of a fruit tree is to grow and bear its fruit each summer, fresh and ripe and delicious. The flesh of the fruit serves to attract humans, animals, and birds, who then pluck the fruit from the tree to carry away to their homes. The fruit provides nutrients and sustenance to many creatures. But it should not be forgotten that within the core of every fruit lies a seed. It is vital to the tree that its seeds be spread far and wide, not just for its own survival, but for the entire cycle of life to continue.

As I looked back on my life now, I realized that I too had been given a very precious seed. I hadn't received just one, however; I had received many. From within the loving orange Light, I was given a seed, and from the hearts of the people who loved me and had helped me, I was given more seeds. As I nurtured them and helped them to grow, the fruits from these seeds in turn nourished me, supported me. And the day I truly allowed my own Light to shine and embraced the gifts I had to share, I had unknowingly brought forth my own fruit to offer the world.

This book is the fruit and within its core lies a seed. It was created to nourish and inspire you on your own journey through life so that you too may offer your greatest gifts to humanity. Whatever it is that you have to bring forth into this world—just bring it. Take a step forward, with faith. Your heart knows the way. Stand tall, be strong, believe in yourself, and allow your own Light to shine. Bear the fruit of your gifts, in whatever way, big or small. In doing so, you too will share a seed—a seed of love.

RESOURCE GUIDE

Visit Cheryl & Brent's online metaphysical store
www.SoulVibes.ca

Coastal Academy of Hypnotic Arts & Science
www.CoastalAcademy.ca

P.T. Mistlberger - Author & Transpersonal Therapist
www.PTMistlberger.com

Tom Dongo - UFO / Paranormal Expert
www.TomDongo.com

Mötesforum Futura - Retreat Center, Sweden
www.Motesforum.se

Kailash Kokopelli - Sound Therapist & Musician
www.Kailash-Kokopelli.com

Atira - Intuitive Reader
www.AtiraPsychic.com

CHERYL ONLINE

Cheryl's Website
www.FractalArt.ca

Play the Path of the Soul Card App on Facebook
www.Apps.FaceBook.com/Oracle_Reading

Cheryl Lee Harnish Fan Page on Facebook
www.FaceBook.com

·✿· GET THE DECK!! ·✿·

Path of the Soul, Destiny Cards
by Cheryl Lee Harnish

ISBN: 9 780978 340706

A 44 Card Deck plus guidebook. Perfect for both self-counsel and professional readings. The cards create stunning spreads and are extremely easy to read and interpret.

Available in most metaphysical stores or online at
www.FractalArt.ca

·✿· GET THE APP! ·✿·

Carry the cards wherever you go!
Now available for your mobile device.

Learn More
www.FractalArt.ca